The Wiley COBOL Syntax Reference Guide: With IBM and VAX Enhancements

GW00418043

Prepared by
NANCY STERN and ROBERT A. STERN

CONTENTS

COBOL Syntax Reference Guide

I. COBOL Character Set

The following lists are in ascending order:

EBCDIC		ASCII	
	space		space
.	period, decimal point	"	quotation mark
<	less than	$	dollar sign
(	left parenthesis	'	single quotation mark
+	plus symbol	(	left parenthesis
$	dollar sign	)	right parenthesis

*	asterisk, multiplication	*	asterisk, multiplication
)	right parenthesis	+	plus symbol
;	semicolon	,	comma
-	hyphen, minus sign	-	hyphen, minus sign
/	slash, division	.	period, decimal point
,	comma	/	slash, division
>	greater than	0–9	digits
'	single quotation mark	;	semicolon
=	equal sign	<	less than
"	quotation mark	=	equal sign
a–z	lowercase letters	>	greater than
A–Z	uppercase letters	A–Z	uppercase letters
0–9	digits	a–z	lowercase letters

II. COBOL Reserved Words

Each COBOL compiler has a list of reserved words that:

1. Includes all entries in the ANS COBOL standard.
2. Includes additional entries not part of the standard but that are either VAX or IBM compiler extensions. These are called enhancements.

The following is based on the 1974 and 1985 American National Standard. You may find that your computer has additional reserved words. Diagnostic messages will print if you are using a reserved word incorrectly.

New reserved words that are not relevant for COBOL 74, but are relevant only for COBOL 85, are denoted with a single asterisk (*). COBOL 74 reserved words that are *not* reserved in the new standard are denoted with a double asterisk (**). Words in red are VAX COBOL 85 extensions. Words in blue are IBM COBOL 85 extensions. Boxed words are both VAX and IBM COBOL 85 extensions.

ACCEPT	CHARACTERS
ACCESS	CLASS *
ACTUAL	CLOCK-UNITS
ADD	CLOSE
ADVANCING	COBOL
AFTER	CODE
ALL	CODE-SET
ALLOWING	COLLATING
ALPHABET *	COLUMN
ALPHABETIC	COM-REG
ALPHABETIC-LOWER *	COMMA
ALPHABETIC-UPPER *	COMMIT
ALPHANUMERIC *	COMMON
ALPHANUMERIC-EDITED *	COMMUNICATION
ALSO	COMP
ALTER	COMP-1
ALTERNATE	COMP-2
AND	COMP-3
ANY *	COMP-4
APPLY	COMP-5
ARE	COMP-6
AREA	COMPUTATIONAL

AREAS
ASCENDING
ASSIGN
AT
AUTHOR
AUTOTERMINATE

BASIS
BATCH
BEFORE
BEGINNING
BELL
BINARY *
BIT
BITS
BLANK
BLINKING
BLOCK
BOLD
BOOLEAN
BOTTOM
BY

CALL
CANCEL
CBL
CD
CF
CH
CHARACTER

COMPUTATIONAL-1
COMPUTATIONAL-2
COMPUTATIONAL-3
COMPUTATIONAL-4
COMPUTATIONAL-5
COMPUTATIONAL-6
COMPUTE
CONCURRENT
CONFIGURATION
CONNECT
CONSOLE
CONTAIN
CONTAINS
CONTENT *
CONTINUE *
CONTROL
CONTROLS
CONVERSION
CONVERTING *
COPY
CORE-INDEX
CORR
CORRESPONDING
COUNT
CURRENCY
CURRENT
CURRENT-DATE

DATA
DATE

4

DATE-COMPILED
DATE-WRITTEN
DAY
DAY-OF-WEEK *
DB
DB-ACCESS-CONTROL-KEY
DB-CONDITION
DB-CURRENT-RECORD-ID
DB-CURRENT-RECORD-NAME
DB-EXCEPTION
DBKEY
DB-KEY
DB-RECORD-NAME
DB-SET-NAME
DB-STATUS
DEBUG-SUB
DB-UWA
DE
DEBUG-CONTENTS
DEBUG-ITEM
DEBUG-LENGTH
DEBUG-LINE
DEBUG-NAME
DEBUG-NUMERIC-CONTENTS
DEBUG-SIZE
DEBUG-START
DEBUG-SUB
DEBUG-SUB-1
DEBUG-SUB-2
DEBUG-SUB-3

ECHO
EGCS
EGI
EJECT
ELSE
EMI
EMPTY
ENABLE
END
END-ACCEPT
END-ADD *
END-CALL *
END-COMMIT
END-COMPUTE *
END-CONNECT
END-DELETE *
END-DISCONNECT
END-DIVIDE *
END-ERASE
END-EVALUATE *
END-FETCH
END-FIND
END-FINISH
END-FREE
END-GET
END-IF *
ENDING
END-KEEP
END-MODIFY
END-MULTIPLY *

DEBUG-SUB-ITEM
DEBUG-SUB-N
DEBUG-SUM-NUM
DEBUGGING
DECIMAL-POINT
DECLARATIVES
DEFAULT
DELETE
DELIMITED
DELIMITER
DEPENDING
DESCENDING
DESCRIPTOR
DESTINATION
DETAIL
DICTIONARY
DISABLE
DISCONNECT
DISP
DISPLAY
DISPLAY-1
DISPLAY-6
DISPLAY-7
DISPLAY-9
DIVIDE
DIVISION
DOES
DOWN
DUPLICATE
DUPLICATES
DYNAMIC

END-OF-PAGE
END-PERFORM *
END-READ *
END-READY
END-RECEIVE *
END-RECONNECT
END-RETURN *
END-REWRITE *
END-ROLLBACK
END-SEARCH *
END-START *
END-STORE
END-STRING *
END-SUBTRACT *
END-UNSTRING *
END-WRITE *
ENTER
ENTRY
ENVIRONMENT
EOP
EQUAL
EQUALS
ERASE
ERROR
ESI
EVALUATE *
EVERY **
EXCEEDS
EXCEPTION
EXCLUSIVE
EXIT

6

EXOR	KEEP
EXTEND	KEY
EXTERNAL *	
	LABEL
FAILURE	LAST
FALSE *	LD
FD	LEADING
FETCH	LEAVE
FILE	LEFT
FILE-CONTROL	LENGTH
FILE-LIMIT	LESS
FILE-LIMITS	LIMIT
FILLER	LIMITS
FINAL	LINAGE
FIND	LINAGE-COUNTER
FINISH	LINE
FIRST	LINE-COUNTER
FOOTING	LINES
FOR	LINKAGE
FREE	LOCALLY
FROM	LOCK
	LOW-VALUE
GENERATE	LOW-VALUES
GET	
GIVING	MATCH
GLOBAL *	MATCHES
GO	MEMBER
GOBACK	MEMBERSHIP
GREATER	MEMORY **
GROUP	MERGE

HEADING
HIGH-VALUE
HIGH-VALUES

ID
IDENTIFICATION
IF
IN
INCLUDING
INDEX
INDEXED
INDICATE
INITIAL
INITIALIZE *
INITIATE
INPUT
INPUT-OUTPUT
INSERT
INSPECT
INSTALLATION
INTO
INVALID
I-O
I-O-CONTROL
IS

JUST
JUSTIFIED

KANJI

MESSAGE
MODE
MODIFY
MODULES **
MORE-LABELS
MOVE
MULTIPLE
MULTIPLY

NATIVE
NEGATIVE
NEXT
NO
NOMINAL
NON-NULL
NONE
NOT
NOTE
NULL
NULLS
NUMBER
NUMERIC
NUMERIC-EDITED

OBJECT-COMPUTER
OCCURS
OF
OFF
OFFSET
OMITTED

8

ON
ONLY
OPEN
OPTIONAL
OR
ORDER *
ORGANIZATION
OTHER *
OTHERS
OUTPUT
OVERFLOW
OWNER

PACKED-DECIMAL *
PADDING *
PAGE
PAGE-COUNTER
PARAGRAPH
PASSWORD
PERFORM
PF
PH
PIC
PICTURE
PLUS
POINTER
POSITION
POSITIVE
PRESENT
PRINTING

REFERENCE-MODIFIER
REFERENCES
REGARDLESS
RELATIVE
RELEASE
RELOAD
REMAINDER
REMOVAL
RENAMES
REPLACE *
REPLACING
REPORT
REPORTING
REPORTS
REREAD
RERUN
RESERVE
RESET
RETAINING
RETRIEVAL
RETURN
RETURN-CODE
REVERSED
REWIND
REWRITE
RF
RH
RIGHT
RMS-FILENAME
RMS-STS

PRIOR
PROCEDURE
PROCEDURES
PROCEED
PROGRAM
PROGRAM-ID
PROTECTED
PURGE *

QUEUE
QUOTE
QUOTES

RANDOM
RD
READ
READERS
READY
REALM
REALMS
RECEIVE
RECONNECT
RECORD
RECORD-NAME
RECORD-OVERFLOW
RECORDING
RECORDS
REDEFINES
REEL
REFERENCE *

RMS-STV
ROLLBACK
ROUNDED
RUN

SAME
SCREEN
SD
SEARCH
SECTION
SECURITY
SEGMENT
SEGMENT-LIMIT
SELECT
SEND
SENTENCE
SEPARATE
SEQUENCE
SEQUENCE-NUMBER
SEQUENTIAL
SERVICE
SET
SETS
SHIFT-IN
SHIFT-OUT
SIGN
SIZE
SKIP-1
SKIP-2
SKIP-3

SORT
SORT-CONTROL
SORT-CORE-SIZE
SORT-FILE-SIZE
SORT-MERGE
SORT-MESSAGE
SORT-MODE-SIZE
SORT-RETURN
SOURCE
SOURCE-COMPUTER
SPACE
SPACES
SPECIAL-NAMES
STANDARD
STANDARD-1
STANDARD-2 *
START
STATUS
STOP
STORE
STRING
SUB-QUEUE-1
SUB-QUEUE-2
SUB-QUEUE-3
SUB-SCHEMA
SUBTRACT
SUCCESS
SUM
SUPPRESS
SYMBOLIC
SYNC

TOP
TRAILING
TRUE *
TYPE

UNDERLINED
UNEQUAL
UNIT
UNLOCK
UNSTRING
UNTIL
UP
UPDATE
UPDATERS
UPON
USAGE
USAGE-MODE
USE
USING

VALUE
VALUES
VARYING

WAIT
WHEN
WHEN-COMPILED
WHERE
WITH
WITHIN
WORDS **

```
SYNCHRONIZED                    WORKING-STORAGE
                                WRITE
TABLE                           WRITE-ONLY
TALLY                           WRITERS
TALLYING
TAPE                            ZERO
TENANT                          ZEROES
TERMINAL                        ZEROS
TERMINATE
TEST                            +
TEXT                            -
THAN                            *
THEN *                          /
THROUGH                         **
THRU                            >
TIME                            <
TIME-OF-DAY                     =
TIMES                           >= *
TITLE                           <= *
TO
```

III. Complete COBOL Language Formats

This guide contains the composite language formats of the American National Standard COBOL. Shaded entries are those that are applicable to COBOL 85 only. Entries in blue are IBM extensions. Entries in red are VAX extensions. Entries with an * are both IBM and VAX extensions.

General Format for IDENTIFICATION DIVISION

$$\left\{\begin{array}{l}\underline{\text{IDENTIFICATION}}\ \underline{\text{DIVISION}}.\\ \underline{\text{ID}}\ \underline{\text{DIVISION}}.\end{array}\right\}$$

PROGRAM-ID. program-name $\left[\text{IS}\ \left\{\begin{array}{l}\underline{\text{COMMON}}\\ \underline{\text{INITIAL}}\end{array}\right\}\ \text{PROGRAM}\right]$.

[AUTHOR. [comment-entry] ...]
[INSTALLATION. [comment-entry] ...]
[DATE-WRITTEN. [comment-entry] ...]
[DATE-COMPILED. [comment-entry] ...]
[SECURITY. [comment-entry] ...]

General Format for ENVIRONMENT DIVISION*

[ENVIRONMENT DIVISION.
[CONFIGURATION SECTION.
[SOURCE-COMPUTER. [computer-name [WITH DEBUGGING MODE].]]
[OBJECT-COMPUTER. [computer-name
    [PROGRAM COLLATING SEQUENCE IS alphabet-name-1]
    [SEGMENT-LIMIT IS segment-number].]]

[SPECIAL-NAMES, [[implementor-name-1

$$\left\{\begin{array}{l} \text{IS mnemonic-name-1} \quad [\underline{\text{ON}} \text{ STATUS IS condition-name-1} \quad [\underline{\text{OFF}} \text{ STATUS IS condition-name-2}]] \\ \text{IS mnemonic-name-2} \quad [\underline{\text{OFF}} \text{ STATUS IS condition-name-2} \quad [\underline{\text{ON}} \text{ STATUS IS condition-name-1}]] \\ \underline{\text{ON}} \text{ STATUS IS condition-name-1} \quad [\underline{\text{OFF}} \text{ STATUS IS condition-name-2}] \\ \underline{\text{OFF}} \text{ STATUS IS condition-name-2} \quad [\underline{\text{ON}} \text{ STATUS IS condition-name-1}] \end{array}\right\} \dots$$

[ALPHABET alphabet-name-1 IS

$$\left\{\begin{array}{l} \text{ASCII} \\ \text{EBCDIC}/ \end{array}\right\}$$

$$\left\{\begin{array}{l} \text{STANDARD-1} \\ \text{STANDARD-2} \\ \underline{\text{NATIVE}} \\ \text{implementor-name-2} \\ \left\{\begin{array}{l} \text{literal-1} \left[\begin{array}{l} \left\{\begin{array}{l} \underline{\text{THROUGH}} \\ \underline{\text{THRU}} \end{array}\right\} \text{literal-2} \\ \{\underline{\text{ALSO}} \text{ literal-3}\} \dots \end{array}\right] \right\} \dots \end{array}\right\} \dots$$

[SYMBOLIC CHARACTERS $\left\{\left\{\text{symbolic-character-1}\right\} \dots \left\{\begin{array}{l} \text{IS} \\ \text{ARE} \end{array}\right\} \{\text{integer-1}\} \dots \right\} \dots$

---

*The ENVIRONMENT DIVISION, CONFIGURATION SECTION, and INPUT-OUTPUT SECTION
entries are required for COBOL 74.

14

$$\left. \left. \begin{array}{l} [\underline{IN}\ \text{alphabet-name-2}] \end{array} \right\} \right]\ \dots$$

$$\left[\underline{CLASS}\ \text{class-name}\ IS \quad \left\{ \text{literal-4} \quad \left[\left\{ \begin{array}{l} \underline{THROUGH} \\ \underline{THRU} \end{array} \right\}\ \text{literal-5} \right] \right\} \dots \right] \dots$$

```
[CURRENCY SIGN IS literal-6]
[DECIMAL-POINT IS COMMA].]]]
[INPUT-OUTPUT SECTION.
FILE-CONTROL.
     {file-control-entry} . . .
[I-O-CONTROL.
```

$$\left[\left[\underline{SAME} \begin{bmatrix} \underline{RECORD} \\ \underline{SORT} \\ \underline{SORT-MERGE} \end{bmatrix} \text{AREA FOR file-name-1} \quad \{\text{file-name-2}\} \dots \right] \dots \right.$$

```
[MULTIPLE FILE TAPE CONTAINS
     {file-name-3 [POSITION integer-1] } . . . ] . . . .]]]]
```

General Format for FILE-CONTROL **Entry**

SEQUENTIAL FILE

SELECT [OPTIONAL] file-name-1

$$\underline{\text{ASSIGN}} \text{ TO} \quad \left\{ \begin{array}{l} \text{implementor-name-1} \\ \text{literal-1} \end{array} \right\} \cdots$$

$$\left[\underline{\text{RESERVE}} \text{ integer-1} \quad \left[\begin{array}{l} \text{AREA} \\ \text{AREAS} \end{array} \right] \right]$$

$$\left[\left[\underline{\text{ORGANIZATION}} \text{ IS} \right] \quad \underline{\text{SEQUENTIAL}} \right]$$

$$\left[\underline{\text{BLOCK}} \text{ CONTAINS} \quad \left[\text{smallest-block } \underline{\text{TO}} \right] \quad \text{blocksize} \quad \left\{ \begin{array}{l} \underline{\text{RECORDS}} \\ \underline{\text{CHARACTERS}} \end{array} \right\} \right]$$

$$\left[\underline{\text{CODE-SET}} \text{ IS} \quad \text{alpha-name} \right]$$

$$\left[\underline{\text{PADDING}} \text{ CHARACTER IS} \quad \left\{ \begin{array}{l} \text{data-name-1} \\ \text{literal-2} \end{array} \right\} \right]$$

$$\left[\underline{\text{RECORD}} \ \underline{\text{DELIMITER}} \text{ IS} \quad \left\{ \begin{array}{l} \underline{\text{STANDARD-1}} \\ \text{implementor-name-2} \end{array} \right\} \right]$$

$$\left[\underline{\text{ACCESS}} \text{ MODE IS} \ \underline{\text{SEQUENTIAL}} \right]$$
$$\left[\text{FILE} \ \underline{\text{STATUS}} \text{ IS} \ \text{data-name-2} \right].$$

RELATIVE FILE

$$\underline{\text{SELECT}} \quad \left[\underline{\text{OPTIONAL}} \right] \quad \text{file-name-1}$$

$$\underline{\text{ASSIGN}} \text{ TO} \quad \left\{ \begin{array}{l} \text{implementor-name-1} \\ \text{literal-1} \end{array} \right\} \cdots$$

$$\left[\underline{\text{RESERVE}} \text{ integer-1} \quad \left[\begin{array}{l} \text{AREA} \\ \text{AREAS} \end{array} \right] \right]$$

16

[ORGANIZATION IS] <u>RELATIVE</u>

$$\left[\underline{BLOCK} \text{ CONTAINS } [\text{smallest-block } \underline{TO}] \quad \text{blocksize} \quad \left\{ \begin{array}{l} \text{RECORDS} \\ \text{CHARACTERS} \end{array} \right\} \right]$$

[PASSWORD IS   data-name]

$$\left[\underline{ACCESS} \text{ MODE IS } \left\{ \begin{array}{l} \underline{SEQUENTIAL} \quad [\underline{RELATIVE} \text{ KEY IS data-name-1}] \\ \left\{ \begin{array}{l} \underline{RANDOM} \\ \underline{DYNAMIC} \end{array} \right\} \quad \underline{RELATIVE} \text{ KEY IS data-name-1} \end{array} \right\} \right]$$

[FILE <u>STATUS</u> IS data-name-2].

INDEXED FILE

<u>SELECT</u>   [OPTIONAL]   file-name-1

$$\underline{ASSIGN} \text{ TO } \left\{ \begin{array}{l} \text{implementor-name-1} \\ \text{literal-1} \end{array} \right\} \ldots$$

$$\left[\underline{RESERVE} \text{ integer-1} \left[\begin{array}{l} \text{AREA} \\ \text{AREAS} \end{array} \right] \right]$$

[ORGANIZATION IS] <u>INDEXED</u>

$$\left[\underline{BLOCK} \text{ CONTAINS } [\text{smallest-block } \underline{TO}] \quad \text{blocksize} \left\{ \begin{array}{l} \text{RECORDS} \\ \text{CHARACTERS} \end{array} \right\} \right]$$

[PASSWORD IS   data-name]

$$\left[\ \underline{ACCESS}\ \text{MODE IS}\ \left\{\begin{array}{l}\underline{SEQUENTIAL}\\\underline{RANDOM}\\\underline{DYNAMIC}\end{array}\right\}\right]$$

$\underline{RECORD}$ KEY IS data-name-1
[$\underline{ALTERNATE}$ $\underline{RECORD}$ KEY IS data-name-2 [WITH $\underline{DUPLICATES}$]] ...
[FILE $\underline{STATUS}$ IS data-name-3].

SORT OR MERGE FILE

$$\underline{SELECT}\ \text{file-name-1}\quad \underline{ASSIGN}\ \text{TO}\ \left\{\begin{array}{l}\text{implementor-name-1}\\\text{literal-1}\end{array}\right\}\ \ldots\ \ .$$

REPORT FILE
$\underline{SELECT}$ [$\underline{OPTIONAL}$] file-name-1

$$\underline{ASSIGN}\ \text{TO}\ \left\{\begin{array}{l}\text{implementor-name-1}\\\text{literal-1}\end{array}\right\}\ \ldots$$

$$\left[\ \underline{RESERVE}\ \text{integer-1}\ \left[\begin{array}{l}\text{AREA}\\\text{AREAS}\end{array}\right]\right]$$

[[$\underline{ORGANIZATION}$ IS] $\underline{SEQUENTIAL}$]

$$\left[\ \underline{BLOCK}\ \text{CONTAINS}\ \text{[smallest-block}\ \underline{TO}\text{]}\ \text{blocksize}\ \left\{\begin{array}{l}\underline{RECORDS}\\\underline{CHARACTERS}\end{array}\right\}\right]$$

[$\underline{CODE-SET}$ IS alpha-name]

18

19

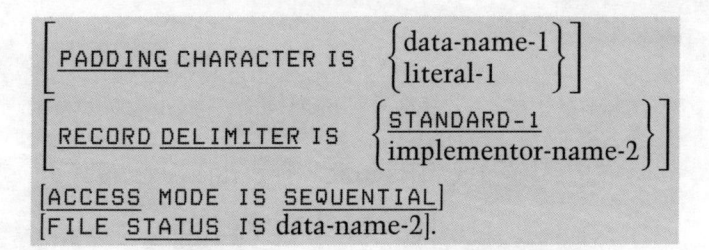

$$\left[\underline{\text{PADDING}} \text{ CHARACTER IS } \left\{ \begin{array}{l} \text{data-name-1} \\ \text{literal-1} \end{array} \right\} \right]$$

$$\left[\underline{\text{RECORD}} \; \underline{\text{DELIMITER}} \text{ IS } \left\{ \begin{array}{l} \underline{\text{STANDARD-1}} \\ \text{implementor-name-2} \end{array} \right\} \right]$$

[<u>ACCESS</u> MODE IS <u>SEQUENTIAL</u>]
[FILE <u>STATUS</u> IS data-name-2].

General Format—I-O-CONTROL

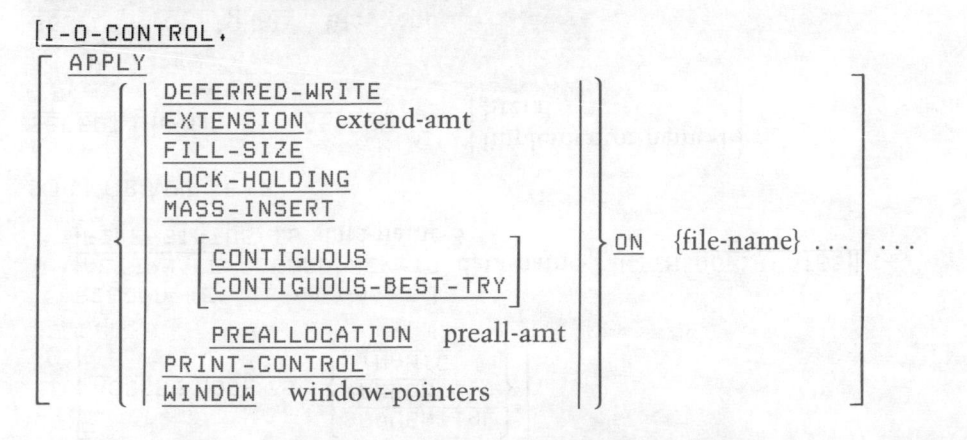

[I-O-CONTROL,
APPLY

- DEFERRED-WRITE
- <u>EXTENSION</u> extend-amt
- FILL-SIZE
- LOCK-HOLDING
- MASS-INSERT

  <u>CONTIGUOUS</u>
  CONTIGUOUS-BEST-TRY

  <u>PREALLOCATION</u> preall-amt
- PRINT-CONTROL
- <u>WINDOW</u> window-pointers

<u>ON</u> {file-name} ... ...

$$\left[\text{; } \underline{\text{RERUN}} \quad \left[\underline{\text{ON}} \quad \left\{ \begin{array}{l} \text{file-name-1} \\ \text{implementor-name} \end{array} \right\} \right] \right.$$

$$\left. \text{EVERY} \quad \left\{ \begin{array}{l} \left\{ \begin{array}{l} \text{[\underline{END} OF]} \quad \left\{ \begin{array}{l} \underline{\text{REEL}} \\ \underline{\text{UNIT}} \end{array} \right\} \\ \text{integer-1} \quad \underline{\text{RECORDS}} \end{array} \right\} \text{ OF } \quad \text{file-name-2} \\ \text{integer-2} \quad \underline{\text{CLOCK-UNITS}} \\ \text{condition-name} \end{array} \right\} \right] \; \ldots$$

$$\left[\text{; } \underline{\text{SAME}} \quad \left[\begin{array}{l} \underline{\text{RECORD}} \\ \underline{\text{SORT}} \\ \underline{\text{SORT-MERGE}} \end{array} \right] \text{ AREA FOR } \quad \text{file-name-3} \quad \{, \text{ file-name-4}\} \; \ldots \right] \; \ldots$$

$$[\text{; } \underline{\text{MULTIPLE FILE}} \text{ TAPE CONTAINS } \text{ file-name-5 } [\underline{\text{POSITION}} \quad \text{integer-3}]$$

$$[, \text{ file-name-6 } [\underline{\text{POSITION}} \quad \text{integer-4}]] \; \ldots \;] \; \ldots \;]].$$

General Format for DATA DIVISION

[DATA DIVISION.
[SUB-SCHEMA SECTION. [subschema-entry [keeplist-entry] ...]]
[FILE SECTION.
[file-description-entry
{record-description-entry} ...] ...
[sort-merge-file-description-entry
{record-description-entry} ...] ...
[report-file-description-entry] ...]

[WORKING-STORAGE SECTION.

$$\begin{bmatrix} \text{77-level-description-entry} \\ \text{record-description-entry} \end{bmatrix} \dots$$]

[LINKAGE SECTION.

$$\begin{bmatrix} \text{77-level-description-entry} \\ \text{record-description-entry} \end{bmatrix} \dots$$]

[COMMUNICATION SECTION.
[communication-description-entry
[record-description-entry] ...] ...]
[REPORT SECTION.
[report-description-entry
{report-group-description-entry} ...] ...]]

General Format—Subschema Description

DB subschema-name WITHIN schema-name

$$\left[\text{FOR database-name} \right] \left[\left\{ \begin{array}{c} \text{THRU} \\ \text{THROUGH} \end{array} \right\} \text{stream-name} \right]$$

General Format—Keeplist Description

LD keeplist-name [LIMIT IS integer].

SEQUENTIAL FILE

<u>FD</u>   file-name-1

[IS EXTERNAL]

[IS GLOBAL]

$$\left[\ \underline{BLOCK}\ CONTAINS\ [integer\text{-}1\ \underline{TO}]\quad integer\text{-}2\quad \begin{Bmatrix} RECORDS \\ CHARACTERS \end{Bmatrix}\right]$$

$$\left[\ \underline{RECORD}\quad \begin{Bmatrix} CONTAINS\ integer\text{-}3\ CHARACTERS \\ IS\ \underline{VARYING}\ IN\ SIZE\ [[FROM\ integer\text{-}4]\ [\underline{TO}\ integer\text{-}5]\ CHARACTERS] \\ [\underline{DEPENDING}\ ON\ data\text{-}name\text{-}1] \\ CONTAINS\ integer\text{-}6\ \underline{TO}\ integer\text{-}7\ CHARACTERS \end{Bmatrix}\right]$$

$$\left[\ \underline{LABEL}\quad \begin{Bmatrix} \underline{RECORD}\ IS \\ \underline{RECORDS}\ ARE \end{Bmatrix}\quad \begin{Bmatrix} \underline{STANDARD} \\ \underline{OMITTED} \end{Bmatrix}\right]$$

$$\left[\ \underline{VALUE}\ \underline{OF}\quad \begin{Bmatrix} implementor\text{-}name\text{-}1\ IS\ \begin{Bmatrix} data\text{-}name\text{-}2 \\ literal\text{-}1 \end{Bmatrix} \end{Bmatrix}\ \ldots\right]$$

$$\left[\ \underline{DATA}\quad \begin{Bmatrix} \underline{RECORD}\ IS \\ \underline{RECORDS}\ ARE \end{Bmatrix}\quad \{data\text{-}name\text{-}3\}\ \ldots\right]$$

$$\left[\ \underline{LINAGE}\ IS\quad \begin{Bmatrix} data\text{-}name\text{-}4 \\ integer\text{-}8 \end{Bmatrix}\quad LINES\quad \left[WITH\ \underline{FOOTING}\ AT\quad \begin{Bmatrix} data\text{-}name\text{-}5 \\ integer\text{-}9 \end{Bmatrix}\right]\right.$$

$$\left.\left[LINES\ AT\ \underline{TOP}\quad \begin{Bmatrix} data\text{-}name\text{-}6 \\ integer\text{-}10 \end{Bmatrix}\right]\left[LINES\ AT\ \underline{BOTTOM}\quad \begin{Bmatrix} data\text{-}name\text{-}7 \\ integer\text{-}11 \end{Bmatrix}\right]\right]$$

[<u>CODE-SET</u> IS alphabet-name-1].
[[<u>ACCESS</u> MODE IS] <u>SEQUENTIAL</u>]
[FILE <u>STATUS</u> IS   file-status].

RELATIVE FILE

<u>FD</u> file-name-1
    [IS <u>EXTERNAL</u>]
    [IS <u>GLOBAL</u>]

$$\left[\underline{BLOCK} \text{ CONTAINS } [\text{integer-1 } \underline{TO}] \quad \text{integer-2} \quad \left\{ \begin{array}{l} \underline{RECORDS} \\ \underline{CHARACTERS} \end{array} \right\} \right]$$

$$\left[\underline{RECORD} \left\{ \begin{array}{l} \text{CONTAINS integer-3 CHARACTERS} \\ \text{IS } \underline{VARYING} \text{ IN SIZE } [[\text{FROM integer-4}] \; [\underline{TO} \text{ integer-5}] \text{ CHARACTERS}] \\ \quad [\underline{DEPENDING} \text{ ON data-name-1}] \\ \text{CONTAINS integer-6 } \underline{TO} \text{ integer-7 CHARACTERS} \end{array} \right\} \right]$$

$$\left[\underline{LABEL} \left\{ \begin{array}{l} \underline{RECORD} \text{ IS} \\ \underline{RECORDS} \text{ ARE} \end{array} \right\} \left\{ \begin{array}{l} \underline{STANDARD} \\ \underline{OMITTED} \end{array} \right\} \right]$$

$$\left[\underline{VALUE} \; \underline{OF} \quad \left\{ \text{implementor-name-1 IS } \left\{ \begin{array}{l} \text{data-name-2} \\ \text{literal-1} \end{array} \right\} \right\} \cdots \right]$$

$$\left[\underline{DATA} \left\{ \begin{array}{l} \underline{RECORD} \text{ IS} \\ \underline{RECORDS} \text{ ARE} \end{array} \right\} \quad \{\text{data-name-3}\} \cdots \right].$$

$$\left[[\underline{ACCESS} \text{ MODE IS}] \left\{ \begin{array}{l} \underline{SEQUENTIAL} \; [\underline{RELATIVE} \text{ KEY IS } \text{ rel-key}] \\ \left\{ \begin{array}{l} \underline{RANDOM} \\ \underline{DYNAMIC} \end{array} \right\} \; \underline{RELATIVE} \text{ KEY IS } \text{ rel-key} \end{array} \right\} \right]$$

[FILE STATUS IS file-status]

INDEXED FILE

FD   file-name-1

    [IS EXTERNAL]

    [IS GLOBAL]

$$\left[\underline{BLOCK} \text{ CONTAINS } [\text{integer-1 } \underline{TO}] \text{ integer-2 } \begin{Bmatrix} \underline{RECORDS} \\ \underline{CHARACTERS} \end{Bmatrix} \right]$$

$$\left[\underline{RECORD} \begin{Bmatrix} \text{CONTAINS integer-3 CHARACTERS} \\ \text{IS } \underline{VARYING} \text{ IN SIZE } [[\text{FROM integer-4}] \ [\underline{TO} \text{ integer-5}] \text{ CHARACTERS}] \\ [\underline{DEPENDING} \text{ ON data-name-1}] \\ \text{CONTAINS integer-6 } \underline{TO} \text{ integer-7 CHARACTERS} \end{Bmatrix} \right]$$

$$\left[\underline{LABEL} \begin{Bmatrix} \underline{RECORD} \text{ IS} \\ \underline{RECORDS} \text{ ARE} \end{Bmatrix} \begin{Bmatrix} \underline{STANDARD} \\ \underline{OMITTED} \end{Bmatrix} \right]$$

$$\left[\underline{VALUE} \ \underline{OF} \begin{Bmatrix} \text{implementor-name-1} & \text{IS} & \begin{Bmatrix} \text{data-name-2} \\ \text{literal-1} \end{Bmatrix} \end{Bmatrix} \cdots \right]$$

$$\left[\underline{DATA} \begin{Bmatrix} \underline{RECORD} \text{ IS} \\ \underline{RECORDS} \text{ ARE} \end{Bmatrix} \text{(data-name-3)} \cdots \right].$$

$$\left[[\underline{ACCESS} \text{ MODE IS}] \begin{Bmatrix} \underline{SEQUENTIAL} \\ \underline{RANDOM} \\ \underline{DYNAMIC} \end{Bmatrix} \right]$$

    RECORD KEY IS   rec-key

    [ALTERNATE RECORD KEY IS alt-key [WITH DUPLICATES]] ...

    [FILE STATUS IS file-status].

SORT-MERGE FILE

<u>SD</u>   file-name-1

$$\left[\underline{RECORD}\begin{Bmatrix}\text{CONTAINS integer-1 CHARACTERS}\\ \text{IS }\underline{VARYING}\text{ IN SIZE [[FROM integer-2] [}\underline{TO}\text{ integer-3] CHARACTERS]}\\ \quad[\underline{DEPENDING}\text{ ON data-name-1]}\\ \text{CONTAINS integer-4 }\underline{TO}\text{ integer-5 CHARACTERS}\end{Bmatrix}\right]$$

$$\left[\underline{DATA}\begin{Bmatrix}\underline{RECORD}\text{ IS}\\ \underline{RECORDS}\text{ ARE}\end{Bmatrix}\{\text{data-name-2}\}\ \dots\right]$$

REPORT FILE

<u>FD</u>   file-name-1
[IS <u>EXTERNAL</u>]
[IS <u>GLOBAL</u>]

$$\left[\underline{BLOCK}\text{ CONTAINS }[\text{integer-1 }\underline{TO}]\quad\text{integer-2}\begin{Bmatrix}\text{RECORDS}\\ \text{CHARACTERS}\end{Bmatrix}\right]$$

$$\left[\underline{RECORD}\begin{Bmatrix}\text{CONTAINS integer-3 CHARACTERS}\\ \text{IS }\underline{VARYING}\text{ IN SIZE [[FROM integer-4] [}\underline{TO}\text{ integer-5] CHARACTERS]}\\ \quad[\underline{DEPENDING}\text{ ON data-name-1]}\\ \text{CONTAINS integer-6 }\underline{TO}\text{ integer-7 CHARACTERS}\end{Bmatrix}\right]$$

$$\left[\underline{LABEL}\begin{Bmatrix}\underline{RECORD}\text{ IS}\\ \underline{RECORDS}\text{ ARE}\end{Bmatrix}\begin{Bmatrix}\underline{STANDARD}\\ \underline{OMITTED}\end{Bmatrix}\right]$$

$$\left[\underline{VALUE}\ \underline{OF}\begin{Bmatrix}\text{implementor-name-1 IS}\begin{Bmatrix}\text{data-name-2}\\ \text{literal-1}\end{Bmatrix}\end{Bmatrix}\ \dots\right]$$

```
[[ACCESS MODE IS]  SEQUENTIAL]
[CODE-SET IS alphabet-name-1]
 ⎰REPORT IS  ⎱  {report-name-1} ...
 ⎱REPORTS ARE⎰
[FILE STATUS IS   file-status].
```

General Format for Data Description Entry

FORMAT 1

$$\text{level-number} \begin{bmatrix} \text{data-name-1} \\ \text{FILLER} \end{bmatrix}$$

```
[REDEFINES data-name-2]
[IS EXTERNAL]
[IS GLOBAL]
```

$$\left[\left\{ \begin{array}{l} \text{PICTURE} \\ \text{PIC} \end{array} \right\} \text{ IS character-string} \right]$$

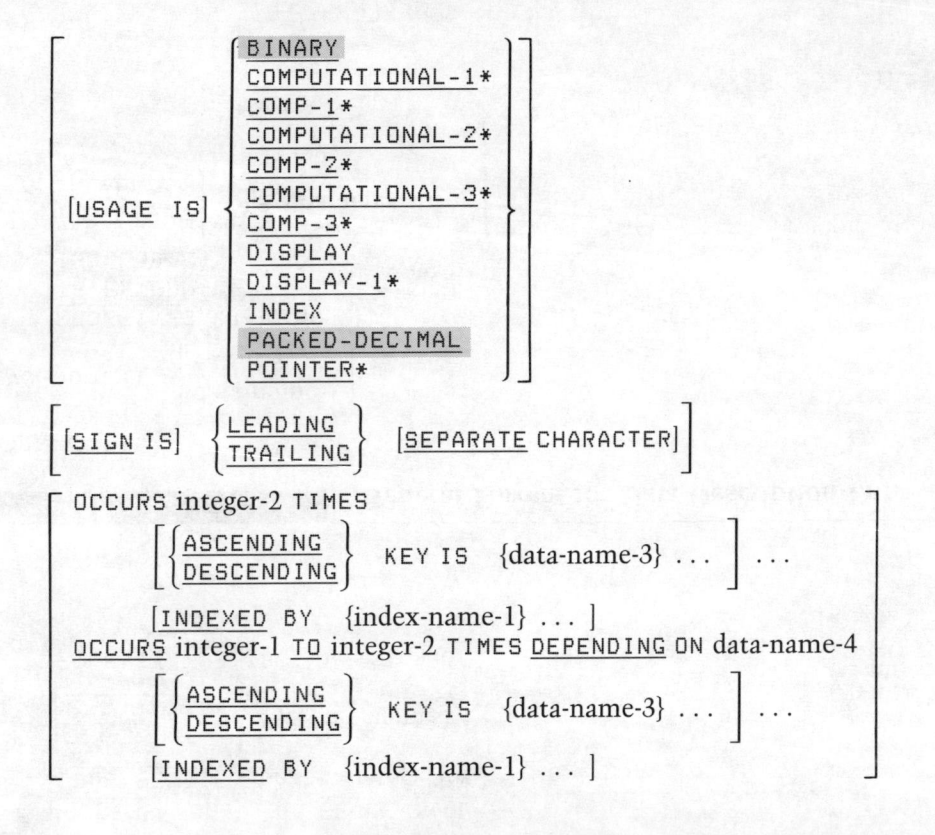

$$[\underline{\text{USAGE}}\ \text{IS}] \left\{ \begin{array}{l} \underline{\text{BINARY}} \\ \underline{\text{COMPUTATIONAL-1}}* \\ \underline{\text{COMP-1}}* \\ \underline{\text{COMPUTATIONAL-2}}* \\ \underline{\text{COMP-2}}* \\ \underline{\text{COMPUTATIONAL-3}}* \\ \underline{\text{COMP-3}}* \\ \underline{\text{DISPLAY}} \\ \underline{\text{DISPLAY-1}}* \\ \underline{\text{INDEX}} \\ \underline{\text{PACKED-DECIMAL}} \\ \underline{\text{POINTER}}* \end{array} \right\}$$

$$\left[[\underline{\text{SIGN}}\ \text{IS}]\ \left\{ \begin{array}{l} \underline{\text{LEADING}} \\ \underline{\text{TRAILING}} \end{array} \right\}\ [\underline{\text{SEPARATE}}\ \text{CHARACTER}] \right]$$

$$\left[\begin{array}{l} \underline{\text{OCCURS}}\ \text{integer-2 TIMES} \\ \quad \left[\left\{ \begin{array}{l} \underline{\text{ASCENDING}} \\ \underline{\text{DESCENDING}} \end{array} \right\}\ \text{KEY IS}\ \{\text{data-name-3}\}\ \dots \right]\ \dots \\ \quad [\underline{\text{INDEXED}}\ \text{BY}\ \{\text{index-name-1}\}\ \dots\ ] \\ \underline{\text{OCCURS}}\ \text{integer-1}\ \underline{\text{TO}}\ \text{integer-2 TIMES}\ \underline{\text{DEPENDING}}\ \text{ON data-name-4} \\ \quad \left[\left\{ \begin{array}{l} \underline{\text{ASCENDING}} \\ \underline{\text{DESCENDING}} \end{array} \right\}\ \text{KEY IS}\ \{\text{data-name-3}\}\ \dots \right]\ \dots \\ \quad [\underline{\text{INDEXED}}\ \text{BY}\ \{\text{index-name-1}\}\ \dots\ ] \end{array} \right]$$

$$
\left[\begin{Bmatrix} \underline{\text{SYNCHRONIZED}} \\ \underline{\text{SYNC}} \end{Bmatrix} \quad \begin{bmatrix} \underline{\text{LEFT}} \\ \underline{\text{RIGHT}} \end{bmatrix} \right]
$$

$$
\left[\begin{Bmatrix} \underline{\text{JUSTIFIED}} \\ \underline{\text{JUST}} \end{Bmatrix} \quad \text{RIGHT} \right]
$$

$$
\left[\underline{\text{BLANK}} \text{ WHEN } \begin{Bmatrix} \underline{\text{ZERO}} \\ \text{ZEROES} \\ \text{ZEROS} \end{Bmatrix} \right]
$$

$$
\left[\underline{\text{VALUE}} \text{ IS } \begin{Bmatrix} \text{literal-1} \\ \underline{\text{EXTERNAL}} \quad \text{external-name} \\ \underline{\text{REFERENCE}} \quad \text{data-name} \\ \text{NULL} \\ \text{NULLS} \end{Bmatrix} \right].
$$

FORMAT 2

66   data-name-1 $\underline{\text{RENAMES}}$ data-name-2 $\left[\begin{Bmatrix} \underline{\text{THROUGH}} \\ \underline{\text{THRU}} \end{Bmatrix} \text{ data-name-3} \right].$

FORMAT 3

88 condition-name-1 $\begin{Bmatrix} \underline{VALUE} \text{ IS} \\ \underline{VALUES} \text{ ARE} \end{Bmatrix}$ $\begin{Bmatrix} \begin{Bmatrix} \text{literal-1} \\ \underline{EXTERNAL} \quad \text{external-name} \\ \underline{REFERENCE} \quad \text{data-name} \\ \text{low-val} \end{Bmatrix} \\ \begin{bmatrix} \begin{Bmatrix} \underline{THROUGH} \\ \underline{THRU} \end{Bmatrix} \begin{Bmatrix} \text{literal-2} \\ \underline{EXTERNAL} \quad \text{external-name} \\ \underline{REFERENCE} \quad \text{data-name} \\ \text{high-val} \end{Bmatrix} \end{bmatrix} \end{Bmatrix}$ ...

FORMAT 1

CD   cd-name-1

```
                          ┌ [[SYMBOLIC QUEUE IS data-name-1]                ┐
                          │    [SYMBOLIC SUB-QUEUE-1 IS data-name-2]         │
                          │    [SYMBOLIC SUB-QUEUE-2 IS data-name-3]         │
                          │    [SYMBOLIC SUB-QUEUE-3 IS data-name-4]         │
                          │    [MESSAGE DATE IS data-name-5]                 │
                          │    [MESSAGE TIME IS data-name-6]                 │
                          │    [SYMBOLIC SOURCE IS data-name-7]              │
    FOR  [INITIAL] INPUT  │    [TEXT LENGTH IS data-name-8]                  │
                          │    [END KEY IS data-name-9]                      │
                          │    [STATUS KEY IS data-name-10]                  │
                          │    [MESSAGE COUNT IS data-name-11]]              │
                          │ [data-name-1, data-name-2, data-name-3,         │
                          │     data-name-4, data-name-5, data-name-6,       │
                          │     data-name-7, data-name-8, data-name-9,       │
                          └     data-name-10, data-name-11]                  ┘
```

30

FORMAT 2

CD cd-name-1 FOR OUTPUT
   [DESTINATION COUNT IS data-name-1]
   [TEXT LENGTH IS data-name-2]
   [STATUS KEY IS data-name-3]
   [DESTINATION TABLE OCCURS integer-1 TIMES
      [INDEXED BY {index-name-1} ...]]
   [ERROR KEY IS data-name-4]
   [SYMBOLIC DESTINATION IS data-name-5].

FORMAT 3

CD cd-name-1

      FOR [INITIAL] I-O
$$\begin{bmatrix} \begin{bmatrix} [\text{MESSAGE DATE IS data-name-1}] \\ [\text{MESSAGE TIME IS data-name-2}] \\ [\text{SYMBOLIC TERMINAL IS data-name-3}] \\ [\text{TEXT LENGTH IS data-name-4}] \\ [\text{END KEY IS data-name-5}] \\ [\text{STATUS KEY IS data-name-6}] \end{bmatrix} \\ [\text{data-name-1, data-name-2, data-name-3,} \\ \text{data-name-4, data-name-5, data-name-6}] \end{bmatrix}$$

General Format for Report Description Entry

RD report-name-1
   [IS GLOBAL]
   [CODE literal-1]

$$\left[\begin{Bmatrix} \underline{\text{CONTROL}} \text{ IS} \\ \underline{\text{CONTROLS}} \text{ ARE} \end{Bmatrix} \begin{Bmatrix} \{\text{data-name-1}\}\dots \\ \underline{\text{FINAL}} \text{ [data-name-1]}\dots \end{Bmatrix}\right]$$

$$\left[\underline{\text{PAGE}} \begin{bmatrix} \text{LIMIT IS} \\ \text{LIMITS ARE} \end{bmatrix} \text{integer-1} \begin{bmatrix} \text{LINE} \\ \text{LINES} \end{bmatrix} \text{[}\underline{\text{HEADING}} \text{ integer-2]}\right.$$

$$\text{[}\underline{\text{FIRST}} \ \underline{\text{DETAIL}} \text{ integer-3]} \quad \text{[}\underline{\text{LAST}} \ \underline{\text{DETAIL}} \text{ integer-4]}$$

$$\left.\text{[}\underline{\text{FOOTING}} \text{ integer-5]}\right].$$

General Format for Report Group Description Entry

FORMAT 1

01   [data-name-1]

$$\left[\underline{\text{LINE}} \text{ NUMBER IS} \begin{Bmatrix} \text{integer-1} \text{ [}\text{ON } \underline{\text{NEXT}} \ \underline{\text{PAGE}}\text{]} \\ \underline{\text{PLUS}} \text{ integer-2} \end{Bmatrix}\right]$$

$$\left[\underline{\text{NEXT}} \ \underline{\text{GROUP}} \text{ IS} \begin{Bmatrix} \text{integer-3} \\ \underline{\text{PLUS}} \text{ integer-4} \\ \underline{\text{NEXT}} \ \underline{\text{PAGE}} \end{Bmatrix}\right]$$

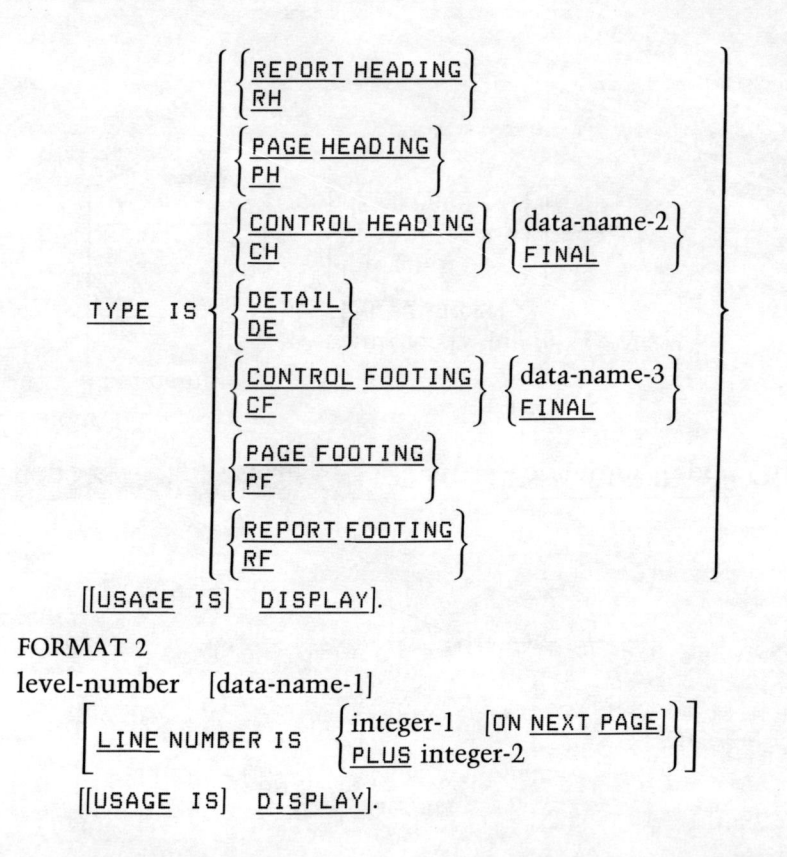

$$
\text{TYPE IS} \left\{
\begin{array}{l}
\left\{\begin{array}{l}\underline{\text{REPORT}}\ \underline{\text{HEADING}}\\ \underline{\text{RH}}\end{array}\right\} \\[4pt]
\left\{\begin{array}{l}\underline{\text{PAGE}}\ \underline{\text{HEADING}}\\ \underline{\text{PH}}\end{array}\right\} \\[4pt]
\left\{\begin{array}{l}\underline{\text{CONTROL}}\ \underline{\text{HEADING}}\\ \underline{\text{CH}}\end{array}\right\}\left\{\begin{array}{l}\text{data-name-2}\\ \underline{\text{FINAL}}\end{array}\right\} \\[4pt]
\left\{\begin{array}{l}\underline{\text{DETAIL}}\\ \underline{\text{DE}}\end{array}\right\} \\[4pt]
\left\{\begin{array}{l}\underline{\text{CONTROL}}\ \underline{\text{FOOTING}}\\ \underline{\text{CF}}\end{array}\right\}\left\{\begin{array}{l}\text{data-name-3}\\ \underline{\text{FINAL}}\end{array}\right\} \\[4pt]
\left\{\begin{array}{l}\underline{\text{PAGE}}\ \underline{\text{FOOTING}}\\ \underline{\text{PF}}\end{array}\right\} \\[4pt]
\left\{\begin{array}{l}\underline{\text{REPORT}}\ \underline{\text{FOOTING}}\\ \underline{\text{RF}}\end{array}\right\}
\end{array}
\right\}
$$

[[USAGE IS] DISPLAY].

FORMAT 2

level-number [data-name-1]

$$
\left[\underline{\text{LINE}}\ \text{NUMBER IS} \left\{\begin{array}{l}\text{integer-1 [ON }\underline{\text{NEXT}}\ \underline{\text{PAGE}}]\\ \underline{\text{PLUS}}\ \text{integer-2}\end{array}\right\}\right]
$$

[[USAGE IS] DISPLAY].

FORMAT 3

level-number   [data-name-1]

$$\left\{ \begin{array}{l} \underline{\text{PICTURE}} \\ \underline{\text{PIC}} \end{array} \right\} \quad \text{IS character-string}$$

[[USAGE IS] DISPLAY]

$$\left[\text{[SIGN IS]} \quad \left\{ \begin{array}{l} \underline{\text{LEADING}} \\ \underline{\text{TRAILING}} \end{array} \right\} \quad \underline{\text{SEPARATE}} \text{ CHARACTER} \right]$$

$$\left[\left\{ \begin{array}{l} \underline{\text{JUSTIFIED}} \\ \underline{\text{JUST}} \end{array} \right\} \quad \text{RIGHT} \right]$$

[BLANK WHEN ZERO]

$$\left[\underline{\text{LINE}} \text{ NUMBER IS } \left\{ \begin{array}{l} \text{integer-1 [ON } \underline{\text{NEXT}} \text{ } \underline{\text{PAGE}}\text{]} \\ \underline{\text{PLUS}} \text{ integer-2} \end{array} \right\} \right]$$

[COLUMN NUMBER IS integer-3]

$$\left\{ \begin{array}{l} \underline{\text{SOURCE}} \text{ IS identifier-1} \\ \underline{\text{VALUE}} \text{ IS literal-1} \\ \{\underline{\text{SUM}} \text{ \{identifier-2\} } \ldots \text{ [}\underline{\text{UPON}} \text{ \{data-name-2\} } \ldots \text{] \} } \ldots \\ \quad \left[\underline{\text{RESET}} \text{ ON } \left\{ \begin{array}{l} \text{data-name-3} \\ \underline{\text{FINAL}} \end{array} \right\} \right] \end{array} \right\}$$

[GROUP INDICATE].

General Format for PROCEDURE DIVISION

FORMAT 1

[PROCEDURE DIVISION [USING {data-name-1} ...] [GIVING identifier-1].
[DECLARATIVES.
{section-name SECTION [segment-number].
USE statement.
[paragraph-name.
[sentence] ...] ... } ...
END DECLARATIVES.]
{section-name SECTION [segment-number].
[paragraph-name.
[sentence] ...] ... } ...]

FORMAT 2

[PROCEDURE DIVISION [USING {data-name-1} ...] [GIVING identifier-1].
{paragraph-name.
[sentence] ... } ...]

General Format for COBOL Verbs

ACCEPT identifier-1 [FROM mnemonic-name-1]
[AT END imperative statement-1]
[NOT AT END imperative statement-2]
[END-ACCEPT]

ACCEPT identifier-2 FROM
$$\begin{cases} \text{DATE} \\ \text{DAY} \\ \text{DAY-OF-WEEK} \\ \text{TIME} \end{cases}$$

ACCEPT   dest-item

FROM LINE NUMBER
$$\begin{cases} \text{line-num} \\ \text{line-id} \quad [\text{PLUS} \quad [\text{plus-num}]] \\ \text{PLUS} \quad [\text{plus-num}] \end{cases}$$

FROM COLUMN NUMBER
$$\begin{cases} \text{column-num} \\ \text{column-id} \quad [\text{PLUS} \quad [\text{plus-num}]] \\ \text{PLUS} \quad [\text{plus-num}] \end{cases}$$

ERASE [TO END OF]
$$\begin{cases} \text{SCREEN} \\ \text{LINE} \end{cases}$$

WITH BELL
UNDERLINED
BOLD
WITH BLINKING

PROTECTED
$$\left[\left\{ \begin{array}{l} \underline{\text{SIZE}} \begin{cases} \text{prot-size-lit} \\ \text{prot-size-item} \end{cases} \\ \text{WITH AUTOTERMINATE} \\ \text{WITH NO BLANK} \\ \text{WITH FILLER prot-fill-lit} \end{array} \right\} \right]$$

```
    ⎡                                                    ⎤ ⎤
    ⎢   WITH CONVERSION                                  ⎥ ⎥
    ⎢   REVERSED                                         ⎥ ⎥
    ⎢   WITH NO ECHO                                     ⎥ ⎥
    ⎢                  ⎧ def-src-lit      ⎫              ⎥ ⎥
    ⎢   DEFAULT IS     ⎨ def-src-item     ⎬              ⎥ ⎥
    ⎢                  ⎩ CURRENT VALUE    ⎭              ⎥ ⎥
    ⎣   CONTROL KEY IN key-dest-item                     ⎦ ⎥

    ⎡ ⎧ [ON EXCEPTION stment] [NOT ON EXCEPTION stment2] ⎫ ⎤
    ⎢ ⎨ [AT END stment] [NOT AT END stment2]             ⎬ ⎥
    ⎣ ⎩                                                  ⎭ ⎦

    [END-ACCEPT]
ACCEPT  CONTROL KEY IN key-dest-item

    ⎧  ⎡                      ⎧ line-num                     ⎫  ⎤  ⎫
    ⎪  ⎢ FROM LINE NUMBER     ⎨ line-id [PLUS [plus-num]]    ⎬  ⎥  ⎪
    ⎪  ⎢                      ⎩ PLUS [plus-num]              ⎭  ⎥  ⎪
    ⎪  ⎢                      ⎧ column-num                   ⎫  ⎥  ⎪
    ⎨  ⎢ FROM COLUMN NUMBER   ⎨ column-id [PLUS [plus-num]]  ⎬  ⎥  ⎬
    ⎪  ⎢                      ⎩ PLUS [plus-num]              ⎭  ⎥  ⎪
    ⎪  ⎢                              ⎧ SCREEN ⎫                ⎥  ⎪
    ⎪  ⎢ ERASE [TO END OF]            ⎨ LINE   ⎬                ⎥  ⎪
    ⎩  ⎣ WITH BELL                    ⎩        ⎭                ⎦  ⎭

    ⎡ ⎧ [ON EXCEPTION stment] [NOT ON EXCEPTION stment2] ⎫ ⎤
    ⎢ ⎨ [AT END stment] [NOT AT END stment2]             ⎬ ⎥
    ⎣ ⎩                                                  ⎭ ⎦
```

[END-ACCEPT]

ACCEPT cd-name-1 MESSAGE COUNT

ADD $\begin{Bmatrix} \text{identifier-1} \\ \text{literal-1} \end{Bmatrix}$ ... TO {identifier-2 [ROUNDED]} ...

[ON SIZE ERROR imperative-statement-1]
[NOT ON SIZE ERROR imperative-statement-2]
[END-ADD]

ADD $\begin{Bmatrix} \text{identifier-1} \\ \text{literal-1} \end{Bmatrix}$ ... TO $\begin{Bmatrix} \text{identifier-2} \\ \text{literal-2} \end{Bmatrix}$

GIVING {identifier-3 [ROUNDED]} ...
[ON SIZE ERROR imperative-statement-1]
[NOT ON SIZE ERROR imperative-statement-2]
[END-ADD]

ADD $\begin{Bmatrix} \text{CORRESPONDING} \\ \text{CORR} \end{Bmatrix}$ identifier-1 TO identifier-2 [ROUNDED]

[ON SIZE ERROR imperative-statement-1]
[NOT ON SIZE ERROR imperative-statement-2]
[END-ADD]

ALTER {procedure-name-1 TO [PROCEED TO] procedure-name-2} ...

CALL $\begin{Bmatrix} \text{identifier-1} \\ \text{literal-1} \end{Bmatrix}$ $\left[\text{USING} \begin{Bmatrix} \text{[BY REFERENCE]} \ \text{\{identifier-2\} ...} \\ \text{BY CONTENT \{identifier-2\} ...} \end{Bmatrix} \cdots \right]$

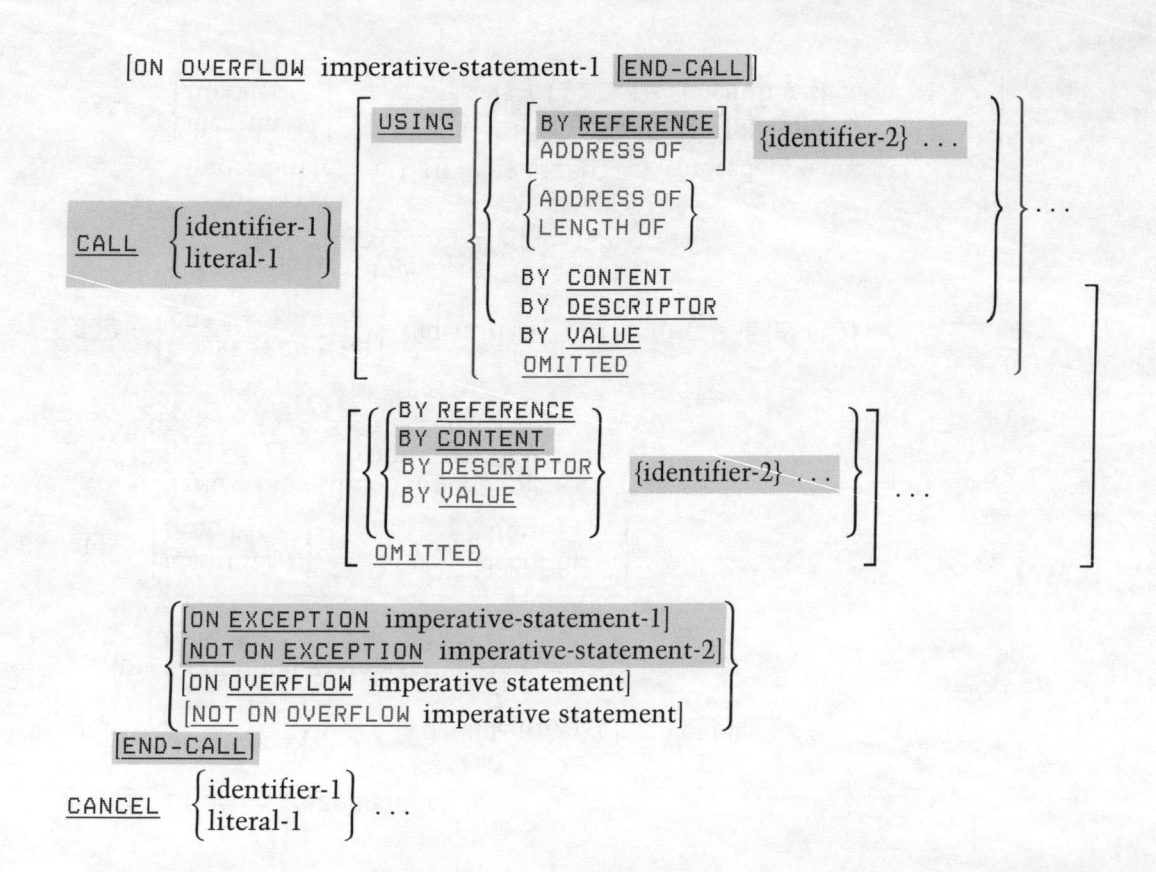

[ON <u>OVERFLOW</u> imperative-statement-1 [END-CALL]]

<u>CALL</u> { identifier-1 / literal-1 }

<u>USING</u>

[BY <u>REFERENCE</u> / ADDRESS OF] {identifier-2} . . .

{ ADDRESS OF / LENGTH OF }

BY <u>CONTENT</u>
BY <u>DESCRIPTOR</u>
BY <u>VALUE</u>
<u>OMITTED</u>

. . .

[{ { BY <u>REFERENCE</u> / BY <u>CONTENT</u> / BY <u>DESCRIPTOR</u> / BY <u>VALUE</u> } {identifier-2} . . . } . . .
<u>OMITTED</u>]

[ON <u>EXCEPTION</u> imperative-statement-1]
[<u>NOT</u> ON <u>EXCEPTION</u> imperative-statement-2]
[ON <u>OVERFLOW</u> imperative statement]
[<u>NOT</u> ON <u>OVERFLOW</u> imperative statement]

[<u>END-CALL</u>]

<u>CANCEL</u> { identifier-1 / literal-1 } . . .

SW CLOSE $\left\{ \text{file-name-1} \left[\begin{Bmatrix} \underline{\text{REEL}} \\ \underline{\text{UNIT}} \end{Bmatrix} \text{[FOR REMOVAL]} \\ \text{WITH} \begin{Bmatrix} \underline{\text{NO REWIND}} \\ \underline{\text{LOCK}} \end{Bmatrix} \right] \right\}$ ...

RI CLOSE {file-name-1 [WITH LOCK]} ...

COMMIT [RETAINING]
    [ON ERROR stment]
    [NOT ON ERROR stment2]
    [END-COMMIT]

COMPUTE {identifier-1 [ROUNDED]} ... $\begin{Bmatrix} = \\ \text{EQUAL} \end{Bmatrix}$ arithmetic-expression-1

    [ON SIZE ERROR imperative-statement-1]
    [NOT ON SIZE ERROR imperative-statement-2]
    [END-COMPUTE]

CONNECT [record-name] TO $\begin{Bmatrix} \{\text{set-name}\} \ldots \\ \underline{\text{ALL}} \end{Bmatrix}$

$\left[\text{RETAINING} \left[\left\{ \left| \begin{matrix} \underline{\text{REALM}} \\ \underline{\text{RECORD}} \\ \underline{\text{SET}} \text{ [set-name]} \ldots \\ \{\text{set-name}\} \ldots \end{matrix} \right| \right\} \right] \text{CURRENCY} \right]$

[ON ERROR stment] [NOT ON ERROR stment2]
[END-CONNECT]

40

```
CONTINUE
DELETE file-name-1 RECORD
     [INVALID KEY imperative-statement-1]
     [NOT INVALID KEY imperative-statement-2]
     [END-DELETE]
```

$$\text{DISABLE} \quad \begin{Bmatrix} \text{INPUT [TERMINAL]} \\ \text{I-O TERMINAL} \\ \text{OUTPUT} \end{Bmatrix} \quad \text{cd-name-1}$$

$$\text{DISCONNECT [record-name] FROM} \quad \begin{Bmatrix} \{\text{set-name}\} \ldots \\ \text{ALL} \end{Bmatrix}$$

```
     [ON ERROR stment]
     [NOT ON ERROR stment2]
     [END-DISCONNECT]
```

$$\text{DISPLAY} \quad \begin{Bmatrix} \text{identifier-1} \\ \text{literal-1} \end{Bmatrix} \ldots \text{[UPON} \begin{Bmatrix} \text{CONSOLE} \\ \text{SYSOUT} \\ \text{mnemonic-name-1} \end{Bmatrix} \quad \text{[WITH NO ADVANCING]}$$

```
DISPLAY {src-item
            ┌ ┌ ┌ AT LINE NUMBER                                        ┐ ┐ ┐
            │ │ │                  ⎧ line-num                       ⎫   │ │ │
            │ │ │                  ⎨ line-id  [PLUS  [plus-num]]     ⎬   │ │ │
            │ │ │                  ⎩ PLUS  [plus-num]               ⎭   │ │ │
            │ │ │ AT COLUMN NUMBER                                      │ │ │
            │ │ │                  ⎧ column-num                     ⎫   │ │ │
            │ │ │                  ⎨ column-id  [PLUS  [plus-num]]   ⎬   │ │ │
            │ │ │                  ⎩ PLUS  [plus-num]               ⎭   │ │ │
            │ ⎨ │ ERASE  [TO END OF]  ⎧ SCREEN ⎫                     ⎬ } ...
            │ │ │                     ⎩ LINE   ⎭                     │ │ │
            │ │ │ WITH BELL                                            │ │ │
            │ │ │ UNDERLINED                                           │ │ │
            │ │ │ BOLD                                                 │ │ │
            │ │ │ WITH BLINKING                                        │ │ │
            │ │ │ REVERSED                                             │ │ │
            └ └ │ WITH CONVERSION                                    ┘ ┘ ┘
       [WITH NO ADVANCING]

DIVIDE  ⎧ identifier-1 ⎫  INTO  ⎧ identifier-2 ⎫  GIVING identifier-3 [ROUNDED]
        ⎩ literal-1    ⎭        ⎩ literal-2    ⎭

       REMAINDER identifier-4
       [ON SIZE ERROR imperative-statement-1]
```

   [NOT ON SIZE ERROR imperative-statement-2]
   [END-DIVIDE]

DIVIDE $\left\{ \begin{array}{l} \text{identifier-1} \\ \text{literal-1} \end{array} \right\}$ BY $\left\{ \begin{array}{l} \text{identifier-2} \\ \text{literal-2} \end{array} \right\}$ GIVING identifier-3 [ROUNDED]

   REMAINDER identifier-4
   [ON SIZE ERROR imperative-statement-1]
   [NOT ON SIZE ERROR imperative-statement-2]
   [END-DIVIDE]

DIVIDE $\left\{ \begin{array}{l} \text{identifier-1} \\ \text{literal-1} \end{array} \right\}$ INTO {identifier-2 [ROUNDED]} ...

   [ON SIZE ERROR imperative-statement-1]
   [NOT ON SIZE ERROR imperative-statement-2]
   [END-DIVIDE]

DIVIDE $\left\{ \begin{array}{l} \text{identifier-1} \\ \text{literal-1} \end{array} \right\}$ INTO $\left\{ \begin{array}{l} \text{identifier-2} \\ \text{literal-2} \end{array} \right\}$

   GIVING {identifier-3 [ROUNDED]} ...
   [ON SIZE ERROR imperative-statement-1]
   [NOT ON SIZE ERROR imperative-statement-2]
   [END-DIVIDE]

DIVIDE $\left\{ \begin{array}{l} \text{identifier-1} \\ \text{literal-1} \end{array} \right\}$ BY $\left\{ \begin{array}{l} \text{identifier-2} \\ \text{literal-2} \end{array} \right\}$

   GIVING {identifier-3 [ROUNDED]} ...
   [ON SIZE ERROR imperative-statement-1]

```
[NOT ON SIZE ERROR imperative-statement-2]
[END-DIVIDE]

ENABLE   ⎧ INPUT [TERMINAL] ⎫   cd-name-1
         ⎨ I-O TERMINAL     ⎬
         ⎩ OUTPUT           ⎭

ENTRY literal USING identifier-1 ...
ERASE [ALL] [record-name]
      [ON ERROR stment]
      [NOT ON ERROR stment2]
      [END-ERASE]

EVALUATE ⎧ identifier-1  ⎫  ALSO ⎧ identifier-2  ⎫ ...
         ⎪ literal-1     ⎪       ⎪ literal-2     ⎪
         ⎨ expression-1  ⎬       ⎨ expression-2  ⎬
         ⎪ TRUE          ⎪       ⎪ TRUE          ⎪
         ⎩ FALSE         ⎭       ⎩ FALSE         ⎭

  {{WHEN

   ⎧ ANY                                                                          ⎫
   ⎪ condition-1                                                                   ⎪
   ⎪ TRUE                                                                          ⎪
   ⎨ FALSE                                                                         ⎬
   ⎪                                                                               ⎪
   ⎪ [NOT] ⎧ identifier-3            ⎫ ⎧ THROUGH ⎫ ⎧ identifier-4            ⎫     ⎪
   ⎩       ⎨ literal-3               ⎬ ⎨ THRU    ⎬ ⎨ literal-4               ⎬     ⎭
           ⎩ arithmetic-expression-1 ⎭ ⎩         ⎭ ⎩ arithmetic-expression-2 ⎭ }}
```

44

```
[ALSO
    ⎧ ANY                                                                              ⎫⎫⎤⎤    ⎫
    ⎪ condition-2                                                                       ⎪⎪⎥⎥    ⎪
    ⎨ TRUE                                                                              ⎬⎬⎥⎥ ...⎬ ...
    ⎪ FALSE                                                                             ⎪⎪⎦⎦    ⎭
    ⎪        ⎧ identifier-5        ⎫ ⎡ ⎧ THROUGH ⎫ ⎧ identifier-6        ⎫ ⎤            ⎪⎪
    ⎩ [NOT] ⎨ literal-5           ⎬ ⎢ ⎨ THRU    ⎬ ⎨ literal-6           ⎬ ⎥            ⎭⎭
             ⎩ arithmetic-expression-3 ⎭ ⎣ ⎩         ⎭ ⎩ arithmetic-expression-4 ⎭ ⎦

    imperative-statement-1} ...
[WHEN OTHER imperative-statement-2]
[END-EVALUATE]
EXIT
EXIT PROGRAM

FETCH database-record
      [FOR UPDATE]

    ⎡                    ⎡ ⎧ ⎧ REALM                 ⎫ ⎫ ⎤                    ⎤
    ⎢                    ⎢ ⎪ ⎪ RECORD                ⎪ ⎪ ⎥                    ⎥
    ⎢ RETAINING          ⎢ ⎨ ⎨ SET [set-name] ...    ⎬ ⎬ ⎥ CURRENCY          ⎥
    ⎣                    ⎣ ⎩ ⎩ {set-name} ...        ⎭ ⎭ ⎦                    ⎦

    ⎡ ⎧ [AT END stment] [NOT AT END stment2]        ⎫ ⎤
    ⎢ ⎨ [ON ERROR stment] [NOT ON ERROR stment2]    ⎬ ⎥
    ⎣ ⎩                                             ⎭ ⎦
[END-FETCH]
```

INITIATE {report-name-1} ...

INSPECT identifier-1 TALLYING

$$
\left\{
\text{identifier-2 FOR}
\left\{
\begin{array}{l}
\text{CHARACTERS} \left[\left\{ \begin{array}{l} \underline{\text{BEFORE}} \\ \underline{\text{AFTER}} \end{array} \right\} \text{INITIAL} \left\{ \begin{array}{l} \text{identifier-4} \\ \text{literal-2} \end{array} \right\} \right] \cdots \\[2em]
\left\{ \begin{array}{l} \underline{\text{ALL}} \\ \underline{\text{LEADING}} \end{array} \right\} \left\{ \begin{array}{l} \text{identifier-3} \\ \text{literal-1} \end{array} \right\} \left[\left\{ \begin{array}{l} \underline{\text{BEFORE}} \\ \underline{\text{AFTER}} \end{array} \right\} \text{INITIAL} \left\{ \begin{array}{l} \text{identifier-4} \\ \text{literal-2} \end{array} \right\} \right] \cdots
\end{array}
\right\} \cdots
\right\} \cdots
$$

INSPECT identifier-1 REPLACING

$$
\left\{
\begin{array}{l}
\underline{\text{CHARACTERS}}\ \underline{\text{BY}} \left\{ \begin{array}{l} \text{identifier-5} \\ \text{literal-3} \end{array} \right\} \left[\left\{ \begin{array}{l} \underline{\text{BEFORE}} \\ \underline{\text{AFTER}} \end{array} \right\} \text{INITIAL} \left\{ \begin{array}{l} \text{identifier-4} \\ \text{literal-2} \end{array} \right\} \right] \cdots \\[3em]
\left\{ \begin{array}{l} \underline{\text{ALL}} \\ \underline{\text{LEADING}} \\ \underline{\text{FIRST}} \end{array} \right\} \left\{ \left\{ \begin{array}{l} \text{identifier-3} \\ \text{literal-1} \end{array} \right\} \underline{\text{BY}} \left\{ \begin{array}{l} \text{identifier-5} \\ \text{literal-3} \end{array} \right\} \left[\left\{ \begin{array}{l} \underline{\text{BEFORE}} \\ \underline{\text{AFTER}} \end{array} \right\} \text{INITIAL} \left\{ \begin{array}{l} \text{identifier-4} \\ \text{literal-2} \end{array} \right\} \right] \cdots \right\} \cdots
\end{array}
\right\} \cdots
$$

INSPECT identifier-1 TALLYING

$$
\left\{
\text{identifier-2 FOR}
\left\{
\begin{array}{l}
\underline{\text{CHARACTERS}} \left[\left\{ \begin{array}{l} \underline{\text{BEFORE}} \\ \underline{\text{AFTER}} \end{array} \right\} \text{INITIAL} \left\{ \begin{array}{l} \text{identifier-4} \\ \text{literal-2} \end{array} \right\} \right] \cdots \\[2em]
\left\{ \begin{array}{l} \underline{\text{ALL}} \\ \underline{\text{LEADING}} \end{array} \right\} \left\{ \begin{array}{l} \text{identifier-3} \\ \text{literal-1} \end{array} \right\} \left[\left\{ \begin{array}{l} \underline{\text{BEFORE}} \\ \underline{\text{AFTER}} \end{array} \right\} \text{INITIAL} \left\{ \begin{array}{l} \text{identifier-4} \\ \text{literal-2} \end{array} \right\} \right] \cdots
\end{array}
\right\} \cdots
\right\} \cdots
$$

REPLACING

$$\left\{ \begin{array}{l} \underline{\text{CHARACTERS}} \ \underline{\text{BY}} \left\{ \begin{array}{l} \text{identifier-5} \\ \text{literal-3} \end{array} \right\} \left[\left\{ \begin{array}{l} \underline{\text{BEFORE}} \\ \underline{\text{AFTER}} \end{array} \right\} \text{INITIAL} \left\{ \begin{array}{l} \text{identifier-4} \\ \text{literal-2} \end{array} \right\} \right] \dots \\[2em] \left\{ \begin{array}{l} \underline{\text{ALL}} \\ \underline{\text{LEADING}} \\ \underline{\text{FIRST}} \end{array} \right\} \left\{ \left\{ \begin{array}{l} \text{identifier-3} \\ \text{literal-1} \end{array} \right\} \underline{\text{BY}} \left\{ \begin{array}{l} \text{identifier-5} \\ \text{literal-3} \end{array} \right\} \left[\left\{ \begin{array}{l} \underline{\text{BEFORE}} \\ \underline{\text{AFTER}} \end{array} \right\} \text{INITIAL} \left\{ \begin{array}{l} \text{identifier-4} \\ \text{literal-2} \end{array} \right\} \right] \dots \right\} \dots \end{array} \right\} \dots$$

$$\underline{\text{INSPECT}} \text{ identifier-1 } \underline{\text{CONVERTING}} \left\{ \begin{array}{l} \text{identifier-6} \\ \text{literal-4} \end{array} \right\} \underline{\text{TO}} \left\{ \begin{array}{l} \text{identifier-7} \\ \text{literal-5} \end{array} \right\}$$

$$\left[\left\{ \begin{array}{l} \underline{\text{BEFORE}} \\ \underline{\text{AFTER}} \end{array} \right\} \text{INITIAL} \left\{ \begin{array}{l} \text{identifier-4} \\ \text{literal-2} \end{array} \right\} \right] \dots$$

$\underline{\text{KEEP}}$ [database-key-id] $\underline{\text{USING}}$ destination-keeplist

[ON $\underline{\text{ERROR}}$ imperative statement-1]
[$\underline{\text{NOT}}$ ON $\underline{\text{ERROR}}$ imperative statement-2]
[$\underline{\text{END-KEEP}}$]

$$\underline{\text{MERGE}} \text{ file-name-1 } \left\{ \text{ON} \left\{ \begin{array}{l} \underline{\text{ASCENDING}} \\ \underline{\text{DESCENDING}} \end{array} \right\} \text{KEY} \ \{\text{data-name-1}\} \dots \right\} \dots$$

[COLLATING $\underline{\text{SEQUENCE}}$ IS alphabet-name-1]
$\underline{\text{USING}}$ file-name-2 {file-name-3} ...

$$\left\{ \begin{array}{l} \underline{\text{OUTPUT PROCEDURE}} \text{ IS procedure-name-1} \left[\left\{ \begin{array}{l} \underline{\text{THROUGH}} \\ \underline{\text{THRU}} \end{array} \right\} \text{ procedure-name-2} \right] \\[1.5em] \underline{\text{GIVING}} \quad \{\text{file-name-4}\} \dots \end{array} \right\}$$

```
MODIFY ⎡ record-name       ⎤
       ⎣ {record-item} ... ⎦

       ⎡           ⎡⎧⎪ REALM               ⎫⎤         ⎤
       ⎢ RETAINING ⎢⎨⎪ RECORD              ⎬⎥ CURRENCY⎥
       ⎢           ⎢⎪⎩⎧SET [set-name] ...⎫  ⎪⎥         ⎥
       ⎣           ⎣ ⎩{set-name} ...     ⎭  ⎭⎦         ⎦

[ON ERROR stment]
[NOT ON ERROR stment2]
[END-MODIFY]

MOVE  ⎧ identifier-1 ⎫  TO  {identifier-2} ...
      ⎩ literal-1    ⎭

MOVE  ⎧ CORRESPONDING ⎫  identifier-1 TO identifier-2
      ⎩ CORR          ⎭

MULTIPLY  ⎧ identifier-1 ⎫  BY {identifier-2 [ROUNDED]} ...
          ⎩ literal-1    ⎭

   [ON SIZE ERROR imperative-statement-1]
   [NOT ON SIZE ERROR imperative-statement-2]
   [END-MULTIPLY]

MULTIPLY  ⎧ identifier-1 ⎫  BY  ⎧ identifier-2 ⎫
          ⎩ literal-1    ⎭      ⎩ literal-2    ⎭
```

```
GIVING {identifier-3 [ROUNDED]} ...
[ON SIZE ERROR imperative-statement-1]
[NOT ON SIZE ERROR imperative-statement-2]
[END-MULTIPLY]
```

```
        ┌ INPUT {file-name-1   [WITH NO REWIND]} ... ┐
        │ OUTPUT {file-name-2  [WITH NO REWIND]} ... │
        │ ┌ ALLOWING                         ┐        │
        │ │        ┌ ┌ NO OTHERS ┐ ┐         │        │
S OPEN  { │        │ │ READERS   │ │         │        } ...
        │ │        { │ WRITERS   │ }         │        │
        │ │        │ │ UPDATERS  │ │         │        │
        │ │        └ └ ALL       ┘ ┘         │        │
        │ └                                  ┘        │
        │ I-O {file-name-3} ...                       │
        └ EXTEND {file-name-4} ...                    ┘
```

```
         ┌ INPUT {file-name-1} ...          ┐
         │ OUTPUT {file-name-2} ...         │
         │ ┌ ALLOWING                ┐      │
         │ │        ┌ ┌ NO OTHERS ┐ ┐ │      │
RI OPEN  { │        │ │ READERS   │ │ │      ... 
         │ │        { │ WRITERS   │ } │      │
         │ │        │ │ UPDATERS  │ │ │      │
         │ │        └ └ ALL       ┘ ┘ │      │
         │ └                        ┘ │      │
         │ I-O {file-name-3} ...      │      │
         └ EXTEND {file-name-4} ...   ┘      ┘
```

W <u>OPEN</u> $\left\{\begin{array}{l}\underline{\text{OUTPUT}}\ \{\text{file-name-1}\ [\text{WITH}\ \underline{\text{NO}}\ \underline{\text{REWIND}}]\}\ \ldots \\ \underline{\text{EXTEND}}\ \{\text{file-name-2}\}\ \ldots \end{array}\right\}\ \ldots$

<u>PERFORM</u> $\left[\text{procedure-name-1}\ \left[\left\{\begin{array}{l}\underline{\text{THROUGH}} \\ \underline{\text{THRU}} \end{array}\right\}\ \text{procedure-name-2} \right] \right]$

[imperative-statement-1 <u>END-PERFORM</u>]

<u>PERFORM</u> $\left[\text{procedure-name-1}\ \left[\left\{\begin{array}{l}\underline{\text{THROUGH}} \\ \underline{\text{THRU}} \end{array}\right\}\ \text{procedure-name-2} \right] \right]$

$\left\{\begin{array}{l}\text{identifier-1} \\ \text{integer-1} \end{array}\right\}$ <u>TIMES</u> [imperative-statement-1 <u>END-PERFORM</u>]

<u>PERFORM</u> $\left[\text{procedure-name-1}\ \left[\left\{\begin{array}{l}\underline{\text{THROUGH}} \\ \underline{\text{THRU}} \end{array}\right\}\ \text{procedure-name-2} \right] \right]$

$\left[\text{WITH}\ \underline{\text{TEST}}\ \left\{\begin{array}{l}\underline{\text{BEFORE}} \\ \underline{\text{AFTER}} \end{array}\right\} \right]$ <u>UNTIL</u> condition-1

[imperative-statement-1 <u>END-PERFORM</u>]

<u>PERFORM</u> $\left[\text{procedure-name-1}\ \left[\left\{\begin{array}{l}\underline{\text{THROUGH}} \\ \underline{\text{THRU}} \end{array}\right\}\ \text{procedure-name-2} \right] \right]$

$\left[\text{WITH}\ \underline{\text{TEST}}\ \left\{\begin{array}{l}\underline{\text{BEFORE}} \\ \underline{\text{AFTER}} \end{array}\right\} \right]$

<u>VARYING</u> $\left\{\begin{array}{l}\text{identifier-2} \\ \text{index-name-1} \end{array}\right\}$ <u>FROM</u> $\left\{\begin{array}{l}\text{identifier-3} \\ \text{index-name-2} \\ \text{literal-1} \end{array}\right\}$

52

$$\text{BY} \left\{ \begin{array}{l} \text{identifier-4} \\ \text{literal-2} \end{array} \right\} \quad \underline{\text{UNTIL}} \text{ condition-1}$$

$$\left[\underline{\text{AFTER}} \quad \left\{ \begin{array}{l} \text{identifier-5} \\ \text{index-name-3} \end{array} \right\} \quad \underline{\text{FROM}} \quad \left\{ \begin{array}{l} \text{identifier-6} \\ \text{index-name-4} \\ \text{literal-3} \end{array} \right\} \right.$$

$$\left. \underline{\text{BY}} \left\{ \begin{array}{l} \text{identifier-7} \\ \text{literal-4} \end{array} \right\} \quad \underline{\text{UNTIL}} \text{ condition-2} \right] \dots$$

[imperative-statement-1 $\underline{\text{END-PERFORM}}$]

$\underline{\text{PURGE}}$ cd-name-1

SRI $\underline{\text{READ}}$ file-name-1 [$\underline{\text{NEXT}}$] RECORD [$\underline{\text{INTO}}$ identifier-1]

$$\left[\begin{array}{l} \underline{\text{REGARDLESS}} \text{ OF LOCK} \\ \\ \underline{\text{ALLOWING}} \left\{ \begin{array}{l} \underline{\text{UPDATERS}} \\ \underline{\text{READERS}} \\ \underline{\text{NO}} \text{ OTHERS} \end{array} \right\} \end{array} \right]$$

[AT $\underline{\text{END}}$ imperative-statement-1]
[$\underline{\text{NOT}}$ AT $\underline{\text{END}}$ imperative-statement-2]
[$\underline{\text{END-READ}}$]

R $\underline{\text{READ}}$ file-name-1 RECORD [$\underline{\text{INTO}}$ identifier-1]

$$\left[\begin{array}{l} \underline{\text{REGARDLESS}} \text{ OF LOCK} \\[6pt] \underline{\text{ALLOWING}} \left\{\begin{array}{l} \underline{\text{UPDATERS}} \\ \underline{\text{READERS}} \\ \underline{\text{NO}} \text{ OTHERS} \end{array}\right\} \end{array}\right]$$

[INVALID KEY imperative-statement-3]

[NOT INVALID KEY imperative-statement-4]

[END-READ]

I READ file-name-1 RECORD   [INTO identifier-1]

    [KEY IS data-name-1]

    [INVALID KEY imperative-statement-3]

    [NOT INVALID KEY imperative-statement-4]

    [END-READ]

READY [realm-name] . . .

$$\left[\text{USAGE-MODE IS} \left\{\begin{array}{l} \left\{\begin{array}{l} \underline{\text{CONCURRENT}} \\ \underline{\text{EXCLUSIVE}} \\ \underline{\text{PROTECTED}} \\ \underline{\text{BATCH}} \end{array}\right\} \left[\left\{\begin{array}{l} \underline{\text{RETRIEVAL}} \\ \underline{\text{UPDATE}} \end{array}\right\}\right] \\[24pt] \left\{\begin{array}{l} \underline{\text{RETRIEVAL}} \\ \underline{\text{UPDATE}} \end{array}\right\} \left[\left\{\begin{array}{l} \underline{\text{CONCURRENT}} \\ \underline{\text{EXCLUSIVE}} \\ \underline{\text{PROTECTED}} \\ \underline{\text{BATCH}} \end{array}\right\}\right] \end{array}\right\}\right]$$

[WITH WAIT]

[ON ERROR imperative statement-1]

[NOT ON ERROR imperative statement-2]

[END-READY]

RECEIVE cd-name-1 $\begin{Bmatrix} \underline{MESSAGE} \\ \underline{SEGMENT} \end{Bmatrix}$ INTO identifier-1

[NO DATA imperative-statement-1]
[WITH DATA imperative-statement-2]
[END-RECEIVE]

RECONNECT [record-name] WITHIN $\begin{Bmatrix} \{set\text{-}name\} \dots \\ \underline{ALL} \end{Bmatrix}$

$\left[\text{RETAINING} \left\{ \left| \begin{Bmatrix} \underline{REALM} \\ \underline{RECORD} \\ \begin{Bmatrix} \underline{SET} \text{ [set-name] } \dots \\ \{set\text{-}name\} \dots \end{Bmatrix} \end{Bmatrix} \right| \right\} \text{CURRENCY} \right]$

[ON ERROR stment]
[NOT ON ERROR stment2]
[END-RECONNECT]
RELEASE record-name-1 [FROM identifier-1]
RETURN file-name-1 RECORD [INTO identifier-1]
    AT END imperative-statement-1
    [NOT AT END imperative-statement-2]
    [END-RETURN]
S REWRITE record-name-1 [FROM identifier-1]
RI REWRITE record-name-1 [FROM identifier-1]
    [ALLOWING NO OTHERS]
    [INVALID KEY imperative-statement-1]

[NOT INVALID KEY imperative-statement-2]
[END-REWRITE]

ROLLBACK
   [ON ERROR stment]
   [NOT ON ERROR stment2]
   [END-ROLLBACK]

$$\text{SEARCH identifier-1} \left[\underline{\text{VARYING}} \begin{Bmatrix} \text{identifier-2} \\ \text{index-name-1} \end{Bmatrix} \right]$$

   [AT END imperative-statement-1]

$$\left\{ \underline{\text{WHEN}} \text{ condition-1} \begin{Bmatrix} \text{imperative-statement-2} \\ \underline{\text{NEXT SENTENCE}} \end{Bmatrix} \right\} \dots$$

[END-SEARCH]

SEARCH ALL identifier-1   [AT END imperative-statement-1]

$$\underline{\text{WHEN}} \begin{Bmatrix} \text{data-name-1} \begin{Bmatrix} \text{IS EQUAL TO} \\ \text{IS =} \end{Bmatrix} \begin{Bmatrix} \text{identifier-3} \\ \text{literal-1} \\ \text{arithmetic-expression-1} \end{Bmatrix} \\ \text{condition-name-1} \end{Bmatrix}$$

$$\left[\underline{\text{AND}} \begin{Bmatrix} \text{data-name-2} \begin{Bmatrix} \text{IS EQUAL TO} \\ \text{IS =} \end{Bmatrix} \begin{Bmatrix} \text{identifier-4} \\ \text{literal-2} \\ \text{arithmetic-expression-2} \end{Bmatrix} \\ \text{condition-name-2} \end{Bmatrix} \right] \dots$$

$$\left\{ \begin{array}{l} \text{imperative-statement-2} \\ \underline{\text{NEXT}}\ \underline{\text{SENTENCE}} \end{array} \right\}$$

[END-SEARCH]

<u>SEND</u> cd-name-1 <u>FROM</u> identifier-1

<u>SEND</u> cd-name-1 [<u>FROM</u> identifier-1] $\left\{ \begin{array}{l} \text{WITH identifier-2} \\ \text{WITH } \underline{\text{ESI}} \\ \text{WITH } \underline{\text{EMI}} \\ \text{WITH } \underline{\text{EGI}} \end{array} \right\}$

$$\left[\left\{ \begin{array}{l} \underline{\text{BEFORE}} \\ \underline{\text{AFTER}} \end{array} \right\} \text{ADVANCING} \left\{ \begin{array}{l} \left\{ \begin{array}{l} \text{identifier-3} \\ \text{integer-1} \end{array} \right\} \left[\begin{array}{l} \text{LINE} \\ \text{LINES} \end{array} \right] \\ \left\{ \begin{array}{l} \text{mnemonic-name-1} \\ \underline{\text{PAGE}} \end{array} \right\} \end{array} \right\} \right]$$

[<u>REPLACING</u> LINE]

<u>SET</u> $\left\{ \begin{array}{l} \text{index-name-1} \\ \text{identifier-1} \end{array} \right\}$ ... <u>TO</u> $\left\{ \begin{array}{l} \text{index-name-2} \\ \text{identifier-2} \\ \text{integer-1} \end{array} \right\}$

<u>SET</u> {index-name-3} ... $\left\{ \begin{array}{l} \underline{\text{UP}}\ \underline{\text{BY}} \\ \underline{\text{DOWN}}\ \underline{\text{BY}} \end{array} \right\}$ $\left\{ \begin{array}{l} \text{identifier-3} \\ \text{integer-2} \end{array} \right\}$

<u>SET</u> $\left\{ \text{{mnemonic-name-1}} ... \underline{\text{TO}} \left\{ \begin{array}{l} \underline{\text{ON}} \\ \underline{\text{OFF}} \end{array} \right\} \right\}$ ...

SET {condition-name-1} ... TO TRUE
SET pointer-id TO REFERENCE OF identifier

SET status-code-id TO $\left\{ \begin{array}{l} \text{SUCCESS} \\ \text{FAILURE} \end{array} \right\}$

SET $\left\{ \begin{array}{l} \text{identifier} \\ \text{ADDRESS OF identifier} \end{array} \right\}$ TO $\left\{ \begin{array}{l} \text{identifier} \\ \text{ADDRESS OF identifier} \\ \text{NULL} \\ \text{NULLS} \end{array} \right\}$

SORT file-name-1 $\left\{ \text{ON} \left\{ \begin{array}{l} \text{ASCENDING} \\ \text{DESCENDING} \end{array} \right\} \text{KEY } \{\text{data-name-1}\} ... \right\}$ ...

[WITH DUPLICATES IN ORDER]
[COLLATING SEQUENCE IS alphabet-name-1]

$\left\{ \begin{array}{l} \text{INPUT PROCEDURE IS procedure-name-1} \quad \left[\left\{ \begin{array}{l} \text{THROUGH} \\ \text{THRU} \end{array} \right\} \text{procedure-name-2} \right] \\ \text{USING \{file-name-2\} ...} \end{array} \right\}$

$\left\{ \begin{array}{l} \text{OUTPUT PROCEDURE IS procedure-name-3} \quad \left[\left\{ \begin{array}{l} \text{THROUGH} \\ \text{THRU} \end{array} \right\} \text{procedure-name-4} \right] \\ \text{GIVING \{file-name-3\} ...} \end{array} \right\}$

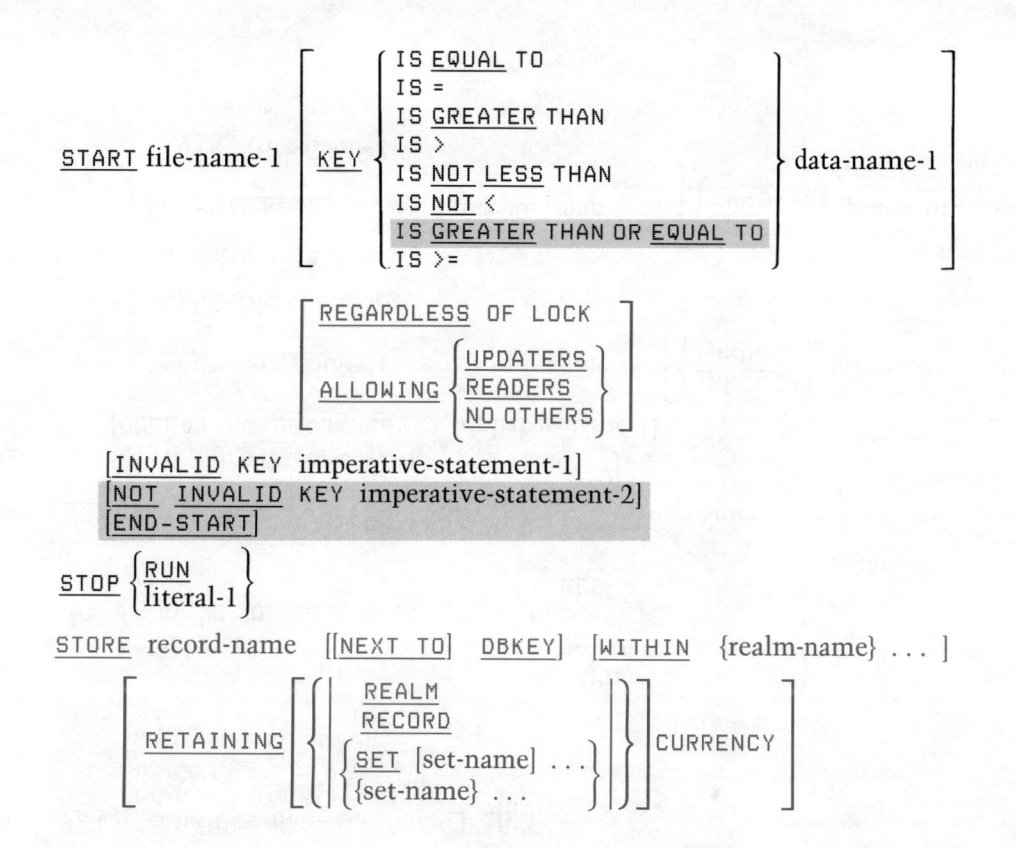

$$\underline{\text{START}} \text{ file-name-1} \left[\underline{\text{KEY}} \begin{Bmatrix} \text{IS } \underline{\text{EQUAL}} \text{ TO} \\ \text{IS } = \\ \text{IS } \underline{\text{GREATER}} \text{ THAN} \\ \text{IS } > \\ \text{IS } \underline{\text{NOT}} \underline{\text{LESS}} \text{ THAN} \\ \text{IS } \underline{\text{NOT}} < \\ \text{IS } \underline{\text{GREATER}} \text{ THAN OR } \underline{\text{EQUAL}} \text{ TO} \\ \text{IS } >= \end{Bmatrix} \right] \text{data-name-1}$$

$$\left[\begin{array}{l} \underline{\text{REGARDLESS}} \text{ OF LOCK} \\ \\ \underline{\text{ALLOWING}} \begin{Bmatrix} \underline{\text{UPDATERS}} \\ \underline{\text{READERS}} \\ \underline{\text{NO}} \text{ OTHERS} \end{Bmatrix} \end{array} \right]$$

[INVALID KEY imperative-statement-1]
[NOT INVALID KEY imperative-statement-2]
[END-START]

$$\underline{\text{STOP}} \begin{Bmatrix} \underline{\text{RUN}} \\ \text{literal-1} \end{Bmatrix}$$

$\underline{\text{STORE}}$ record-name [[NEXT TO] DBKEY] [WITHIN {realm-name} ...]

$$\left[\underline{\text{RETAINING}} \left[\begin{Bmatrix} \begin{Bmatrix} \underline{\text{REALM}} \\ \underline{\text{RECORD}} \\ \underline{\text{SET}} \text{ [set-name] } ... \\ \{\text{set-name}\} ... \end{Bmatrix} \end{Bmatrix} \right] \text{CURRENCY} \right]$$

[ON ERROR stment]
[NOT ON ERROR stment2]
[END-STORE]

STRING $\left\{ \begin{cases} \text{identifier-1} \\ \text{literal-1} \end{cases} \right\} \ldots$ DELIMITED BY $\left\{ \begin{cases} \text{identifier-2} \\ \text{literal-2} \\ \underline{\text{SIZE}} \end{cases} \right\} \ldots$

INTO identifier-3
[WITH POINTER identifier-4]
[ON OVERFLOW imperative-statement-1]
[NOT ON OVERFLOW imperative-statement-2]
[END-STRING]

SUBTRACT $\left\{ \begin{array}{l} \text{identifier-1} \\ \text{literal-1} \end{array} \right\} \ldots$ FROM {identifier-3 [ROUNDED]} ...

[ON SIZE ERROR imperative-statement-1]
[NOT ON SIZE ERROR imperative-statement-2]
[END-SUBTRACT]

SUBTRACT $\left\{ \begin{array}{l} \text{identifier-1} \\ \text{literal-1} \end{array} \right\} \ldots$ FROM $\left\{ \begin{array}{l} \text{identifier-2} \\ \text{literal-2} \end{array} \right\}$

GIVING {identifier-3 [ROUNDED]} ...
[ON SIZE ERROR imperative-statement-1]
[NOT ON SIZE ERROR imperative-statement-2]
[END-SUBTRACT]

SUBTRACT $\left\{\begin{array}{l}\underline{\text{CORRESPONDING}}\\\underline{\text{CORR}}\end{array}\right\}$ identifier-1 FROM identifier-2 [ROUNDED]

    [ON SIZE ERROR imperative-statement-1]
    [NOT ON SIZE ERROR imperative-statement-2]
    [END-SUBTRACT]

SUPPRESS PRINTING

TERMINATE {report-name-1} ...

UNLOCK file-name $\left[\begin{array}{l}\text{RECORD}\\\text{ALL RECORDS}\end{array}\right]$

UNSTRING identifier-1

    $\left[\text{DELIMITED BY [ALL]}\left\{\begin{array}{l}\text{identifier-2}\\\text{literal-1}\end{array}\right\}\left[\text{OR [ALL]}\left\{\begin{array}{l}\text{identifier-3}\\\text{literal-2}\end{array}\right\}\right]\ldots\right]$

    INTO {identifier-4 [DELIMITER IN identifier-5] [COUNT IN identifier-6]} ...
    [WITH POINTER identifier-7]
    [TALLYING IN identifier-8]
    [ON OVERFLOW imperative-statement-1]
    [NOT ON OVERFLOW imperative-statement-2]
    [END-UNSTRING]

USE [GLOBAL] AFTER STANDARD $\left\{\begin{array}{l}\text{EXCEPTION}\\\text{ERROR}\end{array}\right\}$ PROCEDURE ON $\left\{\begin{array}{l}\text{\{file-name-1\} ...}\\\text{INPUT}\\\text{OUTPUT}\\\text{I-O}\\\text{EXTEND}\end{array}\right\}$

USE [GLOBAL] AFTER STANDARD $\begin{Bmatrix} \underline{BEGINNING} \\ \underline{END} \end{Bmatrix}$

$\begin{Bmatrix} FILE \\ REEL \\ UNIT \end{Bmatrix}$ LABEL PROCEDURE ON $\begin{Bmatrix} \text{file-name} \\ \underline{INPUT} \\ \underline{OUTPUT} \\ \underline{I-O} \\ \underline{EXTEND} \end{Bmatrix}$

USE [GLOBAL] BEFORE REPORTING identifier-1

USE FOR DEBUGGING ON $\begin{Bmatrix} \text{cd-name-1} \\ [\underline{ALL} \text{ REFERENCES OF}] \text{ identifier-1} \\ \text{file-name-1} \\ \text{procedure-name-1} \\ \underline{ALL} \underline{PROCEDURES} \end{Bmatrix} \dots$

USE [GLOBAL] FOR DB-EXCEPTION
$\left[ON \begin{Bmatrix} \{DBM\$\_\text{exception-condition}\} \dots \\ \underline{OTHER} \end{Bmatrix} \right]$

S WRITE record-name-1 [FROM identifier-1]
    [ALLOWING NO OTHERS]

$$
\left[\left\{ \begin{array}{l} \underline{BEFORE} \\ \underline{AFTER} \end{array} \right\} \text{ADVANCING} \left\{ \begin{array}{l} \left\{ \begin{array}{l} \text{identifier-2} \\ \text{integer-1} \end{array} \right\} \left[\begin{array}{l} \text{LINE} \\ \text{LINES} \end{array} \right] \\ \left\{ \begin{array}{l} \text{mnemonic-name-1} \\ \underline{PAGE} \end{array} \right\} \end{array} \right\} \right]
$$

$$
\left[\text{AT} \left\{ \begin{array}{l} \underline{END-OF-PAGE} \\ \underline{EOP} \end{array} \right\} \text{imperative-statement-1} \right]
$$

$$
\left[\underline{NOT} \text{ AT} \left\{ \begin{array}{l} \underline{END-OF-PAGE} \\ \underline{EOP} \end{array} \right\} \text{imperative-statement-2} \right]
$$

[END-WRITE]

RI WRITE record-name-1 [FROM identifier-1]

[ALLOWING NO OTHERS]

[INVALID KEY imperative-statement-1]

[NOT INVALID KEY imperative-statement-2]

[END-WRITE]

General Format for Copy and Replace Statements

$$
\underline{COPY} \text{ text-name-1} \left[\left\{ \begin{array}{l} \underline{OF} \\ \underline{IN} \end{array} \right\} \text{library-name-1} \right]
$$

$$\left[\underline{\text{REPLACING}} \left\{ \begin{Bmatrix} \text{==pseudo-text-1==} \\ \text{identifier-1} \\ \text{literal-1} \\ \text{word-1} \end{Bmatrix} \underline{\text{BY}} \begin{Bmatrix} \text{==pseudo-text-2==} \\ \text{identifier-2} \\ \text{literal-2} \\ \text{word-2} \end{Bmatrix} \right\} \dots \right]$$

$\underline{\text{COPY}}$ record-name $\underline{\text{FROM}}$ $\underline{\text{DICTIONARY}}$

$$\left[\begin{array}{l} \underline{\text{REPLACING}} \\ \left\{ \begin{Bmatrix} \text{==pseudo-text-1==} \\ \text{identifier-1} \\ \text{literal-1} \\ \text{word-1} \end{Bmatrix} \underline{\text{BY}} \begin{Bmatrix} \text{==pseudo-text-2==} \\ \text{identifier-2} \\ \text{literal-2} \\ \text{word-2} \end{Bmatrix} \right\} \dots \end{array} \right] .$$

$\underline{\text{REPLACE}}$ {==pseudo-text-1== BY ==pseudo-text-2==} ...

$\underline{\text{REPLACE}}$ $\underline{\text{OFF}}$

General Format for Conditions

RELATION CONDITION

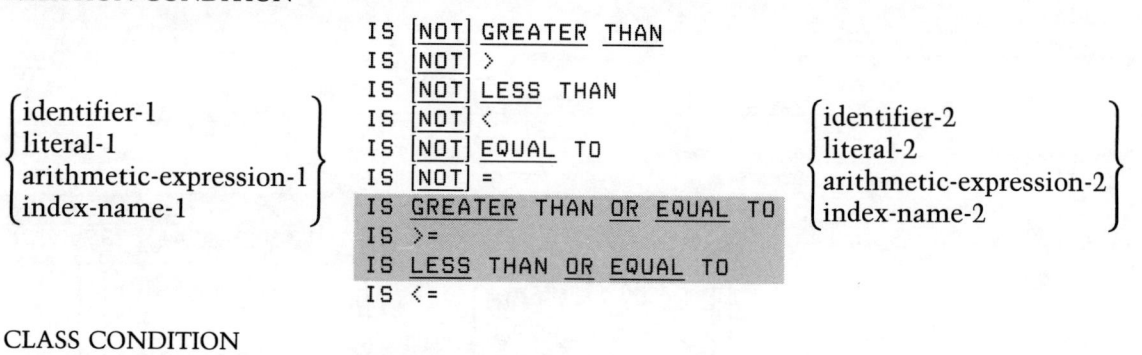

CLASS CONDITION

identifier-1 IS [NOT]
- NUMERIC
- ALPHABETIC
- ALPHABETIC-LOWER
- ALPHABETIC-UPPER
- class-name

CONDITION-NAME CONDITION

condition-name-1

CURRENCY INDICATOR ACCESS

$$\underline{\text{CURRENT}} \left[\text{WITHIN} \begin{Bmatrix} \text{record-name} \\ \text{set-name} \\ \text{realm-name} \end{Bmatrix} \right]$$

KEEPLIST ACCESS

$$\begin{Bmatrix} \underline{\text{OFFSET}} & \text{integer-exp} \\ \underline{\text{FIRST}} & \\ \underline{\text{LAST}} & \end{Bmatrix} \underline{\text{WITHIN}} \text{ keeplist-name}$$

SWITCH-STATUS CONDITION

condition-name-1

SIGN CONDITION

$$\text{arithmetic-expression-1 IS } [\underline{\text{NOT}}] \begin{Bmatrix} \underline{\text{POSITIVE}} \\ \underline{\text{NEGATIVE}} \\ \underline{\text{ZERO}} \end{Bmatrix}$$

TENANCY CONDITION

$$[\underline{\text{NOT}}] \text{ [set-name]} \begin{Bmatrix} \underline{\text{OWNER}} \\ \underline{\text{MEMBER}} \\ \underline{\text{TENANT}} \end{Bmatrix}$$

DATABASE KEY CONDITION

$$\text{database-key IS } [\underline{\text{NOT}}] \begin{Bmatrix} \underline{\text{ALSO}} \text{ database-key} \\ \underline{\text{NULL}} \\ \underline{\text{WITHIN}} \text{ keeplist-name} \end{Bmatrix}$$

SUCCESS/FAILURE CONDITION

status-code-id IS $\left\{ \begin{matrix} \underline{SUCCESS} \\ \underline{FAILURE} \end{matrix} \right\}$

NEGATED CONDITION

<u>NOT</u> condition-1

COMBINED CONDITION

condition-1 $\left\{ \left\{ \begin{matrix} \underline{AND} \\ \underline{OR} \end{matrix} \right\} \text{ condition-2} \right\} \ldots$

ABBREVIATED COMBINED RELATION CONDITION

relation-condition $\left\{ \left\{ \begin{matrix} \underline{AND} \\ \underline{OR} \end{matrix} \right\} \text{ [<u>NOT</u>] [relational-operator] object} \right\} \ldots$

DATABASE KEY IDENTIFIER ACCESS

database-key-identifier

DATABASE SET OWNER ACCESS

<u>OWNER</u> WITHIN set-name

RECORD SEARCH ACCESS

$$\left\{\begin{array}{l} \underline{FIRST} \\ \underline{LAST} \\ \underline{NEXT} \\ \underline{PRIOR} \\ \underline{ANY} \\ \underline{DUPLICATE} \\ \underline{[RELATIVE]} \quad \text{int-exp} \end{array}\right\}$$

[record-name] $\left[\underline{WITHIN} \left\{\begin{array}{l} \text{realm-name} \\ \text{set-name} \end{array}\right\}\right]\left[\begin{array}{l} \underline{USING} \text{ [record-key]} \ldots \\ \underline{WHERE} \text{ [boolean-expression]} \end{array}\right]$

boolean-express:
{boolean-alt [OR boolean-alt] ...}
boolean-alt:
{simple-boolean-relation [AND simple-boolean-relation] ...}
simple-boolean-relation:

$$\left\{\begin{array}{l} \text{boolean-condition} \\ \underline{NOT} \text{ boolean-expression} \end{array}\right\}$$

boolean-condition:

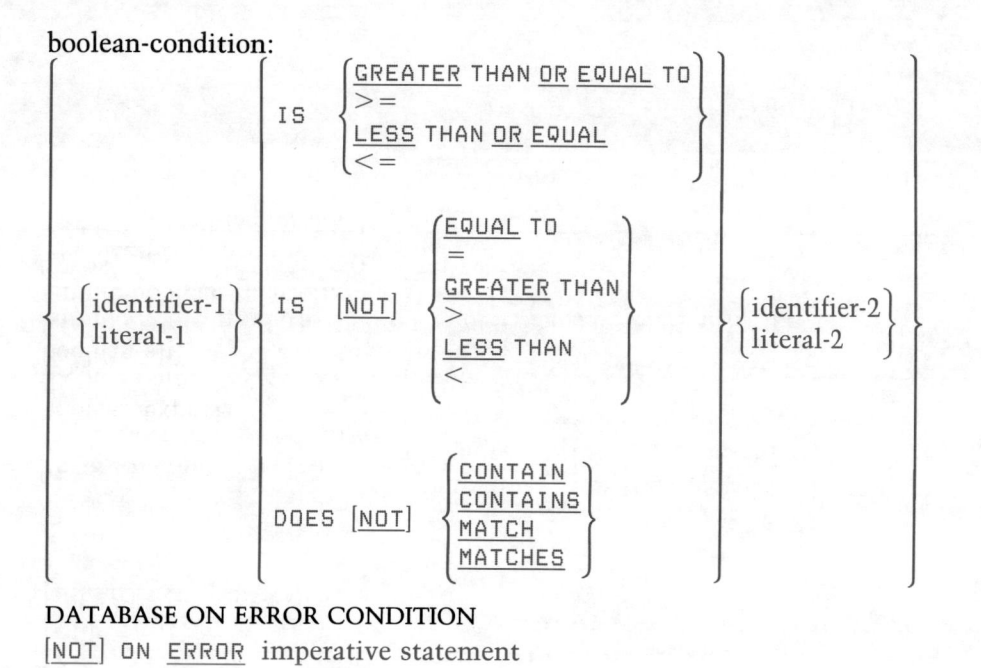

DATABASE ON ERROR CONDITION

[NOT] ON ERROR imperative statement

RETAINING CLAUSE

$$\left[\underline{\text{RETAINING}} \left[\left\{ \left| \begin{array}{l} \underline{\text{REALM}} \\ \underline{\text{RECORD}} \\ \left\{ \begin{array}{l} \underline{\text{SET}} \text{ [set-name]} \dots \\ \{\text{set-name}\} \dots \end{array} \right\} \end{array} \right| \right\} \underline{\text{CURRENCY}} \right] \right]$$

Qualification

FORMAT 1

$$\left\{ \begin{array}{l} \text{data-name-1} \\ \text{condition-name} \end{array} \right\} \left\{ \begin{array}{l} \left\{ \left\{ \begin{array}{l} \underline{\text{IN}} \\ \underline{\text{OF}} \end{array} \right\} \text{data-name-2} \right\} \dots \left[\left\{ \begin{array}{l} \underline{\text{IN}} \\ \underline{\text{OF}} \end{array} \right\} \left\{ \begin{array}{l} \text{file-name} \\ \text{cd-name} \end{array} \right\} \right] \\ \left\{ \begin{array}{l} \underline{\text{IN}} \\ \underline{\text{OF}} \end{array} \right\} \left\{ \begin{array}{l} \text{file-name} \\ \text{cd-name} \end{array} \right\} \end{array} \right\}$$

FORMAT 2

$$\text{paragraph-name} \left\{ \begin{array}{l} \underline{\text{IN}} \\ \underline{\text{OF}} \end{array} \right\} \text{section-name}$$

FORMAT 3

$$\text{text-name} \left\{ \begin{array}{l} \underline{\text{IN}} \\ \underline{\text{OF}} \end{array} \right\} \text{library-name}$$

FORMAT 4

$$\underline{\text{LINAGE-COUNTER}} \quad \left\{\begin{array}{c}\underline{\text{IN}}\\\underline{\text{OF}}\end{array}\right\} \quad \text{report-name}$$

FORMAT 5

$$\left\{\begin{array}{c}\underline{\text{PAGE-COUNTER}}\\\underline{\text{LINE-COUNTER}}\end{array}\right\} \quad \left\{\begin{array}{c}\underline{\text{IN}}\\\underline{\text{OF}}\end{array}\right\} \quad \text{report-name}$$

FORMAT 6

$$\text{data-name-3} \left\{\begin{array}{l}\left\{\begin{array}{c}\underline{\text{IN}}\\\underline{\text{OF}}\end{array}\right\} \quad \text{data-name-4} \quad \left[\left\{\begin{array}{c}\underline{\text{IN}}\\\underline{\text{OF}}\end{array}\right\} \quad \text{report-name}\right]\\\left\{\begin{array}{c}\underline{\text{IN}}\\\underline{\text{OF}}\end{array}\right\} \quad \text{report-name}\end{array}\right\}$$

Miscellaneous Formats

SUBSCRIPTING

$$\left\{\begin{array}{l}\text{condition-name-1}\\\text{data-name-1}\end{array}\right\} \quad \left(\begin{array}{l}\text{integer-1}\\\text{data-name-2 } [\{\pm\} \text{ integer-2}]\\\text{index-name-1 } [\{\pm\} \text{ integer-3}]\\\text{arithmetic-expression}\end{array}\right\} \dots)$$

REFERENCE MODIFICATION

data-name-1 (leftmost-character-position: [length])

IDENTIFIER

$$\text{data-name-1} \quad \left[\begin{Bmatrix} \text{IN} \\ \text{OF} \end{Bmatrix} \text{data-name-2} \right] \quad \dots \quad \left[\begin{Bmatrix} \text{IN} \\ \text{OF} \end{Bmatrix} \begin{Bmatrix} \text{cd-name} \\ \text{file-name} \\ \text{report-name} \end{Bmatrix} \right]$$

[({subscript} . . .)]   [(leftmost-character-position: [length])]

General Format for Nested Source Programs

```
IDENTIFICATION DIVISION.
PROGRAM-ID.  program-name-1 [IS INITIAL PROGRAM].
[ENVIRONMENT DIVISION.  environment-division-content]
[DATA DIVISION.  data-division-content]
[PROCEDURE DIVISION.  procedure-division-content]
[[nested-source-program] . . .
END PROGRAM program-name-1.]
```

General Format for Nested-Source-Program

IDENTIFICATION DIVISION.

PROGRAM-ID.   program-name-2 $\left[\text{IS} \left\{ \left| \dfrac{\text{COMMON}}{\text{INITIAL}} \right| \right\} \text{PROGRAM} \right]$.

[ENVIRONMENT DIVISION. environment-division-content]
[DATA DIVISION. data-division-content]
[PROCEDURE DIVISION. procedure-division-content]
[nested-source-program] . . .
END PROGRAM program-name-2.

General Format for a Sequence of Source Programs

{IDENTIFICATION DIVISION.
PROGRAM-ID.   program-name-3 [IS INITIAL PROGRAM].
[ENVIRONMENT DIVISION. environment-division-content]
[DATA DIVISION. data-division-content]
[PROCEDURE DIVISION. procedure-division-content]
[nested-source-program] . . .
END PROGRAM program-name-3.} . . .
IDENTIFICATION DIVISION.
PROGRAM-ID.   program-name-4 [IS INITIAL PROGRAM].
[ENVIRONMENT DIVISION. environment-division-content]

[DATA DIVISION. data-division-content]
[PROCEDURE DIVISION. procedure-division-content]
[[nested-source-program] ...
  END PROGRAM program-name-4.]

IV. FUNCTION NAMES AVAILABLE IN EXTENSIONS TO COBOL 85

ABS	INTEGER	ORD
ACOS	INTEGER-OF-DATE	ORD-MAX
ANNUITY	INTEGER-OF-DAY	ORD-MIN
ASIN	INTEGER-PART	PI
ATAN	LENGTH	PRESENT-VALUE
CHAR	LENGTH-AN	RANDOM
CHAR-NATIONAL	LOG	RANGE
COS	LOG10	REM
CURRENT-DATE	LOWER-CASE	REVERSE
DATE-OF-INTEGER	MAX	SIGN
DAY-OF-INTEGER	MEAN	SIN
DISPLAY-OF	MEDIAN	SQRT
EXCEPTION-FILE	MIDRANGE	STANDARD-DEVIATION
EXCEPTION-LOCATION	MIN	SUM
EXCEPTION-STATEMENT	MOD	TAN
EXCEPTION-STATUS	NATIONAL-OF	UPPER-CASE
EXP	NUMVAL	VARIANCE
FACTORIAL	NUMVAL-C	WHEN-COMPILED
FRACTION-PART		

V. NEW COBOL 9X RESERVED WORDS

ALIGN	INHERITS	PROPERTY
B-AND	INTERFACE	RAISE
B-NOT	INTERFACE-ID	REPOSITORY
B-OR	INVARIANT	RESERVED
B-XOR	INVOKE	RETURNING
CLASS-ID	METHOD	REUSES
CONFORMING	METHOD-ID	SELF
END-INVOKE	NATIONAL	SUPER
EXCEPTION-OBJECT	NATIONAL-EDITED	SYSTEM-OBJECT
FACTORY	OBJECT	UNIVERSAL
FUNCTION	OVERRIDE	